1 + 1 = 3

A Guide to Developing and Implementing a Winning Business Strategy

Preface

About the Author

Stephen Thomas has 35 years of managerial experience, 15 years as a division or company President/CEO and 20 years as a marketing executive with major U.S. corporations. In addition, he taught Strategic Management (capstone course for graduating seniors), International Business, Organizational Behavior, Consumer Behavior, and International Marketing at Flagler College in St. Augustine, Florida, where he was the faculty chairperson responsible for the development of the college's five-year strategic plan. He ranked in the top quartile of college instructors nationally.

Thomas spent 20 years with Newell Rubbermaid, consisting of more than 20 consumer products manufacturing and marketing independent business units. He was President of five different progressively larger divisions, with his last position as President over eight European companies headquartered in Brussels, Belgium. Newell's primary rapid growth vehicle, throughout the mid-1980's and 1990's, was the acquisition of under-performing consumer products companies with a strong market position, establishing a succinct business strategy, and driving the business to meet minimum Newell aggressive financial performance standards. In the decade of the 1990's, Newell ranked eleventh among Fortune 500 companies in return on stockholder's investment.

Upon leaving Newell, Thomas held two interim President/CEO positions to turn around failing acquisitions. Thomas held a number of marketing managerial positions prior to Newell, including Black and Decker, AMF, and Toastmaster Appliances.

In addition to managing a group of European companies, he has extensive experience sourcing in the Pacific Basin and establishing manufacturing in both Asia and Mexico. The majority of his background was marketing to the big box retailers, both domestic and international (i.e. WalMart, Target, Home Depot, Lowes, Penney's, Carrefour, B&Q, etc.). In addition to specializing in strategy development and implementation, he had a successful track record in new product development and introduction, acquisitions, big box retailer relations, and personnel development.

Thomas holds a B.A. degree in Marketing from the University of Northern Iowa, an M.B.A. in Management from Drake University, with post-masters credits from Penn State University. He has been a guest lecturer to M.B.A. classes at the University of Missouri, The Ohio State University, Arizona State University, and Stetson College. He resides on the Northeast coast of Florida with his wife, Karen. They have three adult children and four grandchildren.

2

About this Guide

In developing *"1 + 1 = 3: A Guide to Developing a Winning Business Strategy,"* the foundation for the guide came from three sources. First, the mentorship of Dr. Robert Katz, a member of the Newell Board of Directors and head of the corporate strategy committee. Dr. Katz taught business strategy at both the Harvard and Stanford business schools. The guidelines and content of the author's 'Strategic Bible' is largely attributable to the format and contents established by Dr. Katz for all Newell business units.

Second, having developed and implemented successful business strategies for a variety of businesses in different industry environments, Thomas established additional criteria and content based on his experience. Third, the guide also reflects current academic thought, much of which was found in the works of Thompson, Peteraf, Gamble, and Strickland (*Crafting and Executing Strategy: The Quest for Competitive Advantage*, McGraw-Hill Irwin, 2012).

The strategy approach presented herein is designed primarily for individual business units or one dimensional organizations. Chapters one through ten relate directly to the development of the actual business strategy for individual business entities. However, there are additional chapters which address international strategies, corporate strategies for diversified organizations, organization and culture, and leadership (from Jim Collins' *Good to Great* and related studies).

Table of Contents

Chapter 1
What is Strategy?

"A company without a strategy is like a ship without a rudder."

To be a successful organization, management must develop, implement, and continuously revise a strategy for directing their business. I have seen company strategies the size of *War and Peace*. How do you communicate and define what is important from a strategy document that weighs 15 pounds? The actual strategy should be no more than eight to ten pages. If more detailed, how do you discern and communicate the key strategic elements to the organization? K.I.S.S. . . . "Keep It Simple Stupid"!

The definition of strategic management contains the following elements:

- Management's action plan for running the business and conducting operations.

- Identifying the competitive moves and business approaches to improve performance and grow the business.

- The umbrella over which directs and unifies the company's various functions toward common goals.

The overriding search is how the company can create competitive advantages in the marketplace that are ***unique, valuable, sustainable, and difficult for competitors to copy.*** There are three ways to create a competitive advantage . . . low cost, differentiation, or a best value (combination of low cost and differentiation). A study of 1,800 firms evidences that those who employ a best value strategy are most frequently the industry leader. Toyota is a good example of a company that employs a best value strategy and they use this strategy as the key element in their aggressive marketing and advertising campaigns. Target is another example of a best value strategy versus WalMart's low cost positioning and the differentiation posture of the upscale department and specialty outlets. These strategic approaches will be discussed in detail later in this guide.

It is imperative to understand that there are two critical elements that a successful strategy must accomplish:

1. **The strategy must improve the firm's profitability and financial condition.**
2. **The strategy must improve the firm's competitive strength and market position.**

A strategy that does not address these two elements will not be successful. Please keep these in mind as we begin developing the strategy document.

Successful strategies should also contain both short-term and long-term elements. What is short-term and what is long-term? It can vary significantly from industry to industry. Consider the pharmaceutical companies . . . their planning horizon can be as much as eight to ten years in order to complete product development, extensive testing, FDA approvals, etc. Conversely, the planning horizon for fashion companies such as Ralph Lauren is less than one year as new seasonal styles are developed and introduced.

Successful strategies must also address the multiple stakeholders of the organization. This includes not only the firm's shareholders and/or investors, but employees, both intermediary customers and end users, suppliers, and the communities in which the firm operates.

The strategy document is not a document to be prepared, put in a desk drawer, and reviewed again in two or three years. The strategy must be a living bible that guides daily activities toward the key strategic objectives. Given the pace of change in today's business environment, generated by technology advancements, globalization of business, changing economic conditions, government regulations, competitive actions, etc., it is recommended that the firm's management team review and update the company strategy every six months. Strategy preparation is not just the job of the firm's chief executive, it is the responsibility of the entire key management team. The firm's key managers, both individually and collectively, should review the current strategy document, retaining some elements, abandoning others, adapting to changes in the business and competitive environment, and creating initiatives to take advantage of new opportunities. Consider the case of the U.S. automobile companies who, between the mid-1980's and the mid-2000's, continued to build and market what was internally convenient under the assumption that we will make and the consumer will buy. They ignored the invasion of Japanese and subsequently Korean automobiles, who were producing vehicles with features and benefits being demanded by consumers. The result . . . a significant loss of market share resulting in financial collapse.

Before beginning the actual discussion of preparing the business strategy, the following is an outline of what I have labeled the "Strategic Bible" . . . the outline of the strategy preparation process that is the basis for the balance of this guide. We will frequently use the fictitious "Acme Widget Company" as an example of various strategic elements.

The Strategic Bible

1. **Strategic Overview**

   A. The Aggregate Market

   B. The Participating Market

   C. Business Definition

   D. Macro Business Environment

   - Economic Variables

   - Demographic Variables

   - Social – Cultural Variables

   - Political and Legal Variables

   - Technological Variables

   - Global Variables

2. **Market Environment**

   A. Industry Environment

   B. Competitive Environment

   C. Five Forces Model of Industry Competitiveness

   D. Key Success Factors (KSFs)

   E. Industry Attractiveness

3. **Company Environment**

   A. Internal Financial Analysis

   B. External Financial Analysis

   C. Sales Analysis

   D. Benchmarking and Best Practices

4. **SWOT Analysis**

   A. Competitive Matrix

   B. Strengths

   C. Weaknesses

   D. Opportunities

   E. Threats

   F. Immediate Action Requirements

5. **Strategic Positioning**

    A. Generic Strategy

    B. Company Vision

    C. Company Mission

    D. New Business Definition (if applicable)

6. **Strategic Objectives**

    A. Revenue and Profit Targets

    B. Strategic Objectives

    C. Action Plans

    D. Timetables

See **APPENDIX A – Strategic Plan Format**

It should be noted that development of the strategy is merely the first step. Once developed and agreed upon by the company's management team, they must:

- Communicate the strategy to the organization.
- Execute the strategy and associated action plans.
- Develop performance objectives and compensation plans to support strategy execution.
- Monitor results and performance.
- Regularly revise and update the strategy.

While the majority of this guide will address the foregoing outline, additional sections are included on international strategies, corporate/diversification strategies, organization and culture, ethical considerations, and leadership.

Chapter 2
The Strategic Overview

The starting point in preparing the business strategy is to understand and document who, what, and where you are. If you don't know who, what, and where you are today, how can you develop tomorrow's expectations?

The Aggregate Market

The **aggregate market** defines the overall global market in which the company participates. For the Acme Widget Company their aggregate market might be simply "Worldwide Widget Market". Why is this important? Management must recognize the difference between the aggregate market for their goods or services versus the market segment or segments in which the firm actually competes. This understanding can lead to expansion opportunities into markets not currently served.

The Participating Market

The **participating market** is the market segment(s) or niche(s) in which the company actually competes. This can be in terms such as products, geography, channels, etc. where the firm conducts their business. The participating market for the Acme Widget Company is "Residential widgets sold through volume retailers and distributors in the United States and Canada". Note the difference between the aggregate market and the participating market. Does this mean the company has an opportunity to expand their focus to include commercial widgets? Market outside the United States and Canada? We'll see . . . that is why we are developing a business strategy designed to enhance both financial and market performance.

Note that the aggregate and participating market are simple and succinct statements. Throughout the development of the strategy, keep in mind that brevity is an attribute.

Business Definition

"If you don't know where you are at, how can you chart your future path?"

This important part of the business strategy is frequently ignored in both the business world and academic community, yet is a critical element in defining the future of the business. The key elements of the business definition are:

- The markets and market segments in which you currently compete.

- The product and/or services in which you are currently involved.

- Your geographic and customer base.

This is important to specify early in strategy development, as analysis of the market and financial variables and the SWOT analysis may suggest that management revise the current business definition.

As an example, when Newell acquired the Kirsch Company, we developed the following business definition:

> *The Kirsch Company is the leading North American manufacturer/importer of a full line of basic and decorative drapery hardware, window shades, and alternative non-textile window treatments for distribution through volume North American retail and commercial channels.*

Exhibit 2 - 1 provides a couple of examples for familiar companies. Keep in mind the statements are those of the author rather than the companies themselves.

Exhibit 2- 1
Sample Strategic Overview Elements

Ford Motor Company:

    Aggregate Market: Worldwide personal and business ground transportation.

    Participating Market: Worldwide personal and business ground transportation.

    Business Definition: Ford is a global manufacturer and marketer of all classes of automobiles and light/medium duty trucks, with the majority of the business centered around North American consumer vehicles.

Southwest Airlines:

    Aggregate Market: Worldwide passenger transportation and air freight.

    Participating Market: North American passenger airline transportation.

    Business Definition: Southwest Airlines is a low cost North American passenger airline offering superior customer service and value.

Note, in the case of Ford, the aggregate market and the participating market are the same. For Southwest, the recent acquisition of Air Tran does add some 'local international' routes to the business definition.

Macro Business Environment

The macro business environment represents those external factors, influences, and events in the world around us that have or will impact our industry and company. These variables are outside the

10

boundaries of the industry and company, over which we have little ability to control or predict. These variables can be quite different from company to company and industry to industry.

As shown in the outer ring in **Exhibit 2 -2**, the macro business environment can be categorized into seven subsets. The following are examples of each.

Economic Variables:	Interest rates; unemployment; inflation; fuel prices; credit availability; loss of retirement savings, etc.
Demographic Variables:	Graying of the workforce and consumers, population shift to warmer climates; growth in the Hispanic population; later and childless marriages; growth of single person households, etc.
Cultural Variables:	Women in professional/managerial roles; women college graduates (57%); increase in temporary workers; fitness; healthy and organic eating; gays in the workforce; environmental sensitivity; two working household heads; acceptance of foreign manufactured products, etc.
Political/Legal Variables:	ADA, OSHA, EPA, FTC, FAA, etc. requirements; minimum wages; business and personal tax rates; future of health care; future of social security; Sarbanes-Oxley Act expansion, etc.
Technology Variables:	Mobile communications; tablet computing; GPS; internet retailing; tax on internet sales; internet information availability; smartphones; nano Technologies, etc.

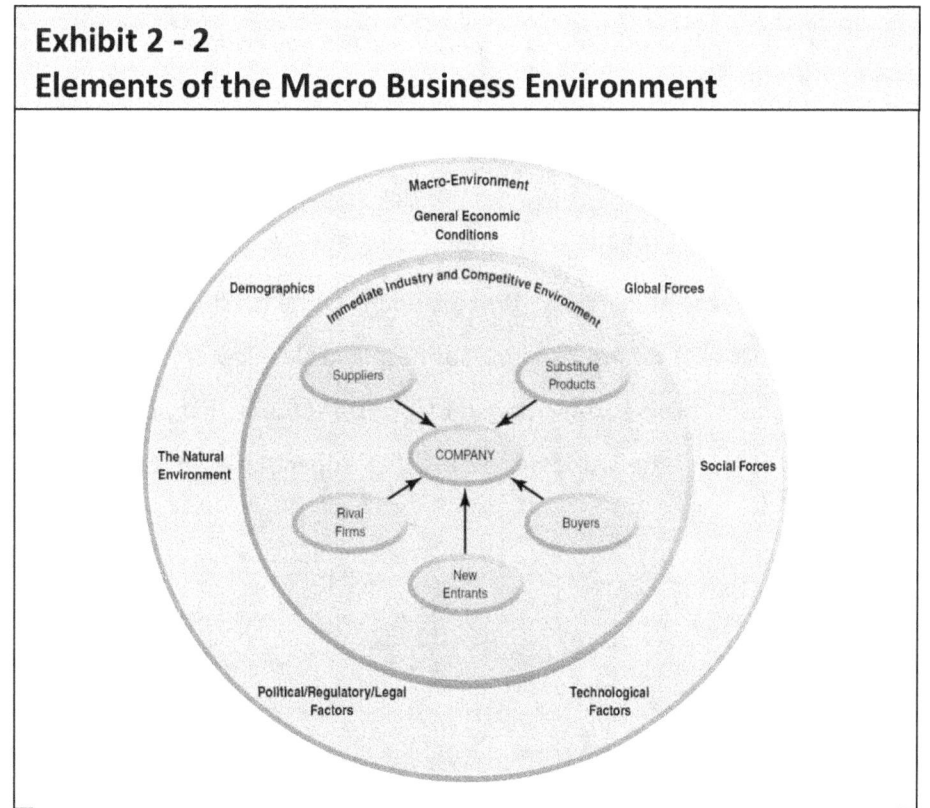

Exhibit 2 - 2
Elements of the Macro Business Environment

Global Variables:	Business globalization; exchange rate fluctuations; terrorism; condition of European and Japanese economies; slowing of growth in the BRIC countries; regional trade agreement expansion; sale of U.S. companies to foreign investors, etc.
Environmental Variables:	Alternative fuels; wind/other alternative energy sources; consumer awareness and practices; conservation mandates, etc.

The following are several examples of how the macro business environment has or can impact business strategies:

- The 2008-09 economic recession impact on the housing and automobile industries.

- In southern and mountain states Costco offers two Coca Cola formulas . . . the typical U.S. formula and a Hispanic formula that is sweeter and utilizes pure sugar cane.

- Grocery stores continue to expand both Hispanic and Asian food sections in response to changing demographics. Several chains are testing all Hispanic product formats in Hispanic dense population areas.

- The influence of higher fuel prices on the product sales mix of the automobile manufacturers.

- New health care regulations are driving lower full-time and more part-time employment.

- Vacation destinations, cruise lines, and airlines have strong marketing programs aimed at the gay population (gays vacation 50% more than straights and spend 50% more when vacationing).

- The technological displacement of CD and DVD retailers, FM radio stations, and newspapers.

- Philip Morris's decision to split tobacco operations into two companies . . . one for North America and one for International. North American tobacco sales are declining, while tobacco consumption throughout Asia, Central and Eastern Europe, and the Middle East is growing. And, if a major class action suit is awarded in the United States, the international company assets are protected.

- Health and obesity concerns and the demise of Hostess (i.e. Twinkies).

Examples such as these are endless. What happens in the macro business environment can and does have a major impact on how we conduct business and develop and implement future business strategies. Again, the macro business environment factors are those that are not industry or company specific . . . they are factors in the world around us that impact how we conduct current and future business.

Chapter 3
The Market (External) Environment

"If you know your enemies and know yourself, you can win a

hundred battles without a single loss."

Sun Tzu, *The Art of War*

You will note from the 'Strategic Bible' outline presented in Chapter 1, a substantial portion of strategy development involves the search for and analysis of both empirical and observational information. In many cases, managers will find that once the information and brutal facts are understood, the strategic objectives to improve market and financial positions become self-evident. We will begin this process by evaluating the market or external environment, which includes understanding the industry and competitive conditions, performing the five forces analysis, identifying the industry's key success factors, and ascertaining the attractiveness of the industry itself.

There is a proliferation of examples of companies who only considered their internal environment versus understanding the market environment. What did Ford and GM do between 1985 and 2005 in response to foreign auto market shares? How well did music stores, including Best Buy and Circuit City (R.I.P.), respond to iTunes and audio streaming? How did Barnes and Noble (R.I.P.) respond to eReaders and tablets? How about Hostess and healthy eating trends? How many families are still purchasing hard bound encyclopedias for $2,000 (like we did)?

With the rapid change in technology, globalization, legislation, etc., if you do not recognize and respond to changes in market and customer demands, you will become a buggy whip like several of the above companies. Business strategies must be dynamic, flexible, and frequently updated in order to respond to these changes.

Industry Environment

Unlike the macro business environment, the industry environment represents what is specifically taking place in the firm's industry. The following questions should be addressed in defining the overall industry environment.

A. What trends, events, and conditions in our industry impact participants? For example, the following are a few of the industry environment elements in the current airline industry:

- Low or no profitability; bankruptcies.
- Mergers and acquisitions, resulting in larger and fewer national competitors with consolidation cost reduction opportunities.
- Continued poor customer service evaluations.
- Prevalence of online ticket purchasing and a multitude of booking websites; results in reduction of brand loyalty.
- Fluctuating fuel costs (fuel is the single largest expense of airline companies).
- Ala carte passenger charges (seating, baggage, food and beverage, pillows, overhead space, etc.).
- Obsolete and congested airport facilities; shortage of air traffic controllers.
- Constant array of new government environmental and security requirements.
- Bio fuel potential.
- Dissatisfied employees; strong union environments.
- Passenger bill of rights.
- Impact of safety lapses and mechanical issues.

B. What is the size and composition of the industry? Historic and future revenue profit and revenue growth?

C. What are the key trends, events, and demands of customers? With end users? With trade/intermediary customers? With suppliers?

D. What is the industry life cycle stage? Early adaption, growth, maturity, saturation or decline?

Competitive Environment

Simply stated, you need to know as much about your main competitors as you know about yourself. Consider a baseball analogy. It's the ninth inning and the score is tied. A left-handed batter steps to the plate with a left-handed pitcher on the mound. The hitter is batting .320 versus right-handed pitchers, but only .220 against left-handers. So, what does the manager do? He brings in a right-handed batter who hit .300 versus lefties. What does the opposing manager do? He brings in a right-handed pitcher who opposing right-handed batters only hit .200. And, the manager instructs the pitcher to keep the ball inside, where the batter frequently strikes out. But, the batter hits .400 when the pitcher throws low and away.

If we have this detailed competitive knowledge in a baseball game, shouldn't we have the same scouting reports and knowledge in a business environment?

Exhibit 3 - 1 suggests using a matrix format to prepare this information, keeping in mind the variables in the vertical column can change from industry to industry. In most instances, evaluating the firm's top three competitors is sufficient. Sales and marketing personnel, with input from other functional areas, should have the knowledge to accurately complete the matrix. Industry trade shows, internet sources, 10k filings, and company websites (CAUTION!) are also potential sources. As will be presented in Chapter 5, for public companies, I have found that _morningstar.com_ is the best source for financial and related information for public companies.

Exhibit 3 – 1 Major Competitor Analysis			
	Competitor A	**Competitor B**	**Competitor C**
Size (Revenue $)			
Products/Services			
Market Share			
Channels Served			
Major Customers			
Target Market			
Geographic Coverage			
Strategy; Likely Actions			
Strengths			
Weaknesses			

Exhibit 3 – 2 provides a sample list regarding the specific characteristics we should know regarding our major competitors.

Exhibit 3 – 2 What You Should Know About Your Primary Competitors

o Sales and market share by category, channel, etc.
o Sales by key customer
o Income statement and balance sheet
o Pricing
o Product and/or service costs
o Strategic direction; objectives
o Management and organization strength
o Product composition (value engineering)
o Facilities . . . location, capacity, automation

o Labor costs
o Quality . . . real and perceived
o Customer service on time, line-fill
o Brand recognition and preference
o Marketing . . . advertising, merchandising, packaging, public relations
o Overall strengths (things to overcome)
o Overall weaknesses (opportunities to attack)

In addition to knowledge of our competition, we need to know the same type of information regarding our major suppliers, trade customers (i.e. intermediaries) and, of course, end users. With respect to trade customers, we must also know who the decision makers are, their expectations, and their credit worthiness. We also must never forget that most transactions are people selling to people. Let's use Target Stores as an example. One of the first things I ask a sales manager for Target is how is your buyer evaluated and compensated. The typical response was "Hell, I don't know." Unacceptable! If you know how the Target buyer is evaluated and compensated, you can design a program that maximizes both the buyer's evaluation and compensation. Your goal should be to help get he or she promoted. And, guess what? You now have a friend for life higher in the Target organization, which can become an insurance policy against competitive threats.

Companies need to ensure that their suppliers of raw materials, components, etc. are financially healthy and have the capabilities of supplying the quantities required on a just-in-time (JIT) basis. In addition, you must demand confidentiality. More than once we have had suppliers that sell both to our firm and to our competition say to us "Do you know that competitor A is doing this, this, and that." This is a major red flag . . . if they are providing this kind of information to us, what kind of information about us are they providing to our competitor?

If you are marketing to intermediaries, such as WalMart or Home Depot, you must know as much, if not more, about the end use purchaser than does the intermediary. You need to understand the demographics, shopping preferences, merchandise expectations, and key purchase criteria. Is the primary criteria price? Selection? Quality? Fashion? Service? Brand? These factors can be very different among even the closest of competitors.

Take, for example, frequent WalMart and Target shoppers. The average household income of a WalMart shopper is about $45,000, compared to nearly $70,000 for the frequent Target shopper. Do you offer the same products, product mix, merchandising, displays, price points, etc.? Of course not. The same applies to Lowes versus Home Depot . . . a large portion of Lowe's shoppers are female, while Home Depot's emphasis is on contractors and heavy DIYers. Accordingly, your marketing mix must be quite different from customer to customer, even though they can be regarded as major competitors.

Five Forces Model of Industry Competitiveness

One of the more popular methods of evaluating the competitiveness of an industry is the **Five Forces Model**. The company should rate each of the five forces shown in **Exhibit 3 – 3** as being **strong, moderate or weak** in order to guide strategic direction, including whether to remain in or exit from an industry or market segment, increase or decrease resource commitments and spending, adjust pricing, and whether protective competitive barriers should be erected. In performing this analysis, be sure to include both traditional competitors as well as potential new, non-traditional competitors (like internet retailing!).

1. The Threat of New Entrants

If new competitors enter your industry, they have the potential to erode revenues and profits of existing competitors. It is unlikely, however, that new firms enter an industry that have:

- High entry costs and/or investments
- Significant economies of scale
- Slow or stagnant demand
- Unhealthy profitability
- Powerful competitors and strong brands
- High levels of product or service differentiation
- High buyer switching costs
- Patents and proprietary technologies

Conversely, the threat of new entrants is strong when these variables are opposite . . . low entry costs, high levels of profitability, weak competitors, etc.

Exhibit 3 – 3
The Five Forces Model of Industry Competitiveness

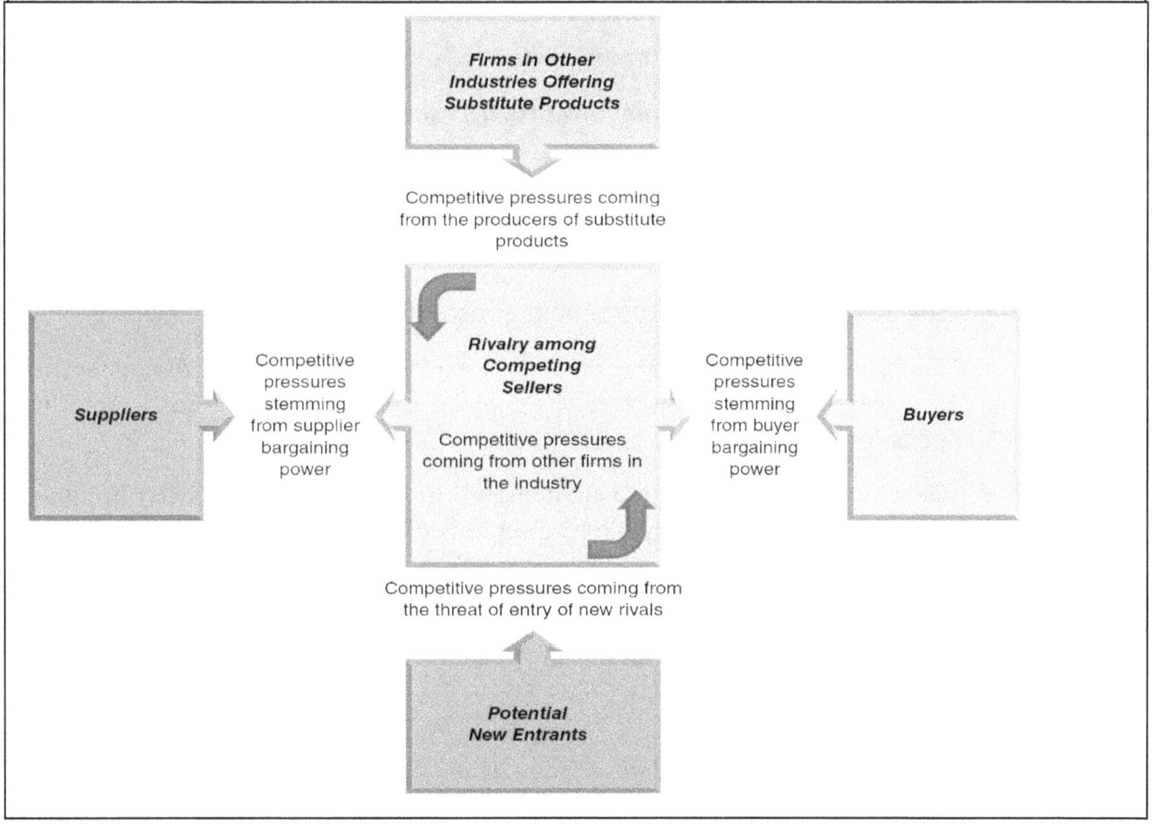

2. The Bargaining Power of Buyers

The stronger the buying power of buyers, the more difficult it will be to generate profits. In many instances, there is more than one buyer in the supply chain, and firms must ensure that the requirements of multiple buyers are addressed. Take, for instance, the grocery trade, where manufacturers sell their product to grocery wholesalers, who in turns sells to a retail grocery chains, who then markets to end using consumers. While you may have product with strong consumer appeal, if you are unable to satisfy the wholesaler, or the wholesaler is not motivated to sell to the retailer, the consumer will never see the product.

Strong buyers threaten an industry and its participants by forcing down prices, bargaining for higher quality or more services, and pitting competitors against each other. Following are conditions and examples where buyers exhibit strong buying power:

- **Large or only a few buyers** . . . for many companies, as much as 30 to 40 percent of their revenue can be generated by single customers like WalMart in general merchandise and Home Depot in DIY products. In order to protect your position, when they say "jump," you reply "how high?"

- **Weak demand** . . . the automobile market during the 2008 - 2009 recession.

- **Undifferentiated and commodity products** with many alternative sellers.

- **Weak brands**; no brand loyalty.

- **Highly reliant suppliers** . . . if the buyer is your largest customer, they have significant power.

- **Low switching costs** . . . little or no buyer cost to change sources of supply.

- **Threat of backward integration** . . . the buyer's firm can enter the market for the products or services you supply, as in the case of Anheiser Busch entering the manufacture of aluminum cans.

- **Direct importation** . . . if you are manufacturing through a third party (frequently in the Pacific Basin), your buyer may elect to work directly with the foreign firm.

- **Information availability** . . . consumers now have increased power over automobile dealers via pricing, features, availability, etc. due to information availability on the internet.

3. Buying Power of Suppliers

Suppliers are those firms that provide input such as raw materials, components, equipment, and special services in the development and construction of the firm's product or service. Suppliers can exert power by raising prices, reducing quality, restricting supply, delaying deliveries, etc.

Suppliers have significant power over your firm when:

- The product or service is in short supply.
- There are only a few suppliers.
- The supplier's product is differentiated and/or there are no substitutes.
- Your firm's cost to switch sources of supply is financially prohibitive.
- Your firm is a small customer for the supplier.
- There is a threat the supplier will forward integrate (i.e. becoming a competitor in your market or industry).
- The supplier's product or service is crucial to your firm.
- The supplier has captive technology and/or patents.

In the early 1980s, DuPont developed *Teflon* non-stick coating for household cooking products, which became an important consumer feature. Since *Teflon* was patent protected, DuPont took advantage to raise prices at will, allocate supply, and deliver when convenient. This continued for several years until competing firms were able to circumvent DuPont's patents, at which time DuPont lost significant market share as they had alienated their customer base. Also consider the power that Microsoft and Intel have over the computer manufacturers.

Seldom do firms have significant supplier power over largest purchasers of their product or service. Apple is an interesting example of having power over big box retailers. WalMart, Target, Best Buy, etc. must carry iPhones, iPods, and iPads, because if they do not, consumers will walk across the street and purchase from a competing retailer. Proctor and Gamble, Coke and Pepsi, and the beer producers also use "pull" marketing strategies through intensive product advertising. If there is high consumer demand, retailers are forced to carry the supplier's product.

Labor unions can also be considered a supplier of people, and, in many industries, they can have substantial power over a firm's operations.

As we have discussed the power of buyers and suppliers, The "Thomas Hypocritical Rule of Buying and Selling" is worth mentioning. If you are the buyer, you need to have secondary sources of supply to protect your firm from potential supplier financial failure, acts of God, catastrophic failures, etc. And, you can pit suppliers against one another to get the best possible concessions. If a hurricane strikes the facilities of a key supplier, and you have no backup source, your firm can be out of business for a significant period of time. Conversely, if I am the supplier, I want to be the single source of supply to my customers . . . I do not want to share the business with a competitor.

4. **Threat of Substitute Products or Services**

If there are easily substitutable products or services that are readily available and offer attractive prices, low switching costs, equivalent performance, and acceptable quality, the firm's business can be in jeopardy. The substitute does not necessarily have to be from traditional competitors or substitutes. Firms must consider potential new or non-traditional substitutes. Several examples of firms who did not recognize a new substitute competitor that adversely impacted their business include:

- Satellite radio and audio streaming vs. traditional AM and FM radio stations
- Videoconferencing vs. airline travel
- Mobile phones vs. land telephone lines
- Digital vs. 35mm cameras
- Email vs. FAX machines, traditional mail
- Laser surgery vs. contact lenses vs. eyeglasses
- Internet vs. TV news vs. newspapers

5. **Intensity of Rivalry Among Competitors (the strongest of the Five Forces)**

It is no surprise that the more intense the competitive rivalry, the lower the profit opportunity. **PRICE** is most frequently the driving force that intensifies a rivalry. Other factors that promote strong rivalry include numerous and/or equally balanced competitors, slow industry growth, excess industry capacity, excess inventories, lack of differentiation between competitors, low switching costs, high barriers to exit the industry, and actions of last breath competitors attempting to remain alive. Drive down any thoroughfare in any U.S. city and you will find McDonald's, Burger King, Wendy's, Taco Bell, KFC, Arby's and a variety of other fast food establishments. The intensity of the rivalry for the consumer's fast food dollar is very intense.

Typical strategies to overcome intense rivalries are listed below:

- Lower prices
- Differentiate your product or service
- Offer higher quality
- Offer a wider selection
- Strengthen the depth and breadth of distribution
- Offer superior customer service
- Innovate . . . offer exclusive and new products or programs
- Build brand image and loyalty through advertising and merchandising
- Acquire or merge with a competitor

We should keep these alternative strategies in mind as we continue and begin development of the firm's SWOT analysis and strategic objectives and action plans.

6. **The Impact of Compliments**

Compliments are product or services that rely on the sales or ownership of other products or services. It is imperative for marketers to know if the firm's products or services are a primary purchase or a secondary purchase. While gasoline is a secondary purchase, gas price increases drove the sales of the Toyota Prius. To develop drapery hardware, you must understand the trends in curtains and draperies. Why is there virtually no frozen food in China? One, there are few refrigerated delivery trucks and two, most homes do not have freezers. Initially, sales via the internet were slow to take hold in China even though 30% of the population utilize the internet. Only 5% of the population own credit cards and home deliveries are erratic. Strategists must understand how compliments and secondary products impact their business models.

In summation, let's evaluate the Five Forces Model in the domestic commercial passenger airline industry. Keep in mind these evaluations are somewhat subjective and there are no right or wrong evaluations.

Threat of New Entrants . . . Low
> High cost of entry; strong competitors; stagnant demand; nominal or no profitability; expanding government regulations

Bargaining Power of Buyers . . . Moderate
> Low in secondary markets, high in major markets; no passenger negotiating power; no switching costs; little differentiation; internet booking yields lowest price selection

Bargaining Power of Suppliers . . . High
> No control over fuel costs; limited number of aircraft suppliers; airports control gates, schedules, costs, etc.; absence of substitutes for longer distances; strong unions

Threat of Substitute Products . . . Moderate to Low
> Don't go; autos; trains; more private jets for rent; video conferencing replacement for business air travel

Intensity of Rivalry . . . High
> Price is #1 success factor; numerous and strong competitors; nominal profit opportunity; mergers and consolidations reducing costs per passenger mile; few ways to differentiate; mature life cycle; no switching costs; high exit barriers

Key Success Factors (KSFs)

Exhibit 3 - 4 displays the most common key success factors.

Exhibit 3 – 4 Typical Industry Key Success Factors (KSFs)		
• Price	• Brand	• Cost
• Advertising	• Quality	• Features
• Innovation	• Technology	• Service
• Location	• Scale Economies	• Selection
• Manufacturing	• Distribution	• Financial Strength
• Style / Fashion	• Patents/Trademarks	

KSFs are those five to seven factors that are most important in order to be successful in a given industry. In almost all instances, price/cost is one of the primary variables.

If we return to the passenger airline industry, the following are potential KSFs:

- Prices / Costs, including surcharges
- Load Factors (i.e. percent of seats filled)
- Locations Served
- Time Schedules
- On Time Arrivals and Departures
- Ease of Transactions
- Average Ground Time
- Customer Service
- Safety
- Comfort

Industry Attractiveness

Based on the foregoing analysis and evaluations, is the industry in which your firm competes (or is contemplating entering) attractive or unattractive? The stronger the competitive forces, the more difficult it will be to earn attractive profits. The market and company environment review should answer the following questions:

- What is the firm's profit potential?

- What is the firm's growth potential, both in revenue and market share?

- How significant is the risk and uncertainty?

- Are competitors vulnerable or weak or is the industry comprised of strong competitors?

- Does the firm have the strength and resources to be successful?

- As a result of the market and competitive evaluation, what is our best strategy?

- If your firm was not currently competing in this industry, would you invest the financial and other resources necessary to enter?

If we evaluate these answers relative to the domestic commercial passenger airline industry, I believe one could conclude that it is **not an attractive opportunity** unless your firm is already a market participant. And, if the firm is already a participant, the opportunity to earn attractive profits is somewhat limited in an uncertain industry environment.

Chapter 4
Basic Financial Analysis for Business Strategies

In preparation for evaluating the internal environment of the firm, basic financial analysis is required. In order to avoid paralysis by analysis, we will be reviewing both the firm's financial data and that of competition from 10,000 feet, avoiding the minutiae unless further explanation of trends or comparisons is required. Actual examples of this analysis are detailed in Chapter 5.

To avoid confusion, several term definitions should be clarified. Sales and revenue are used interchangeably, as are income and profit. Operating income or operating profit is defined as income/profit from operations before interest, taxes, depreciation, and amortization. Net income or net profit refers to income generated after the foregoing.

The Four Basic Rules

1. **Common Size Income Statements**

   Convert all income statement line items to a percent of total or net sales. For comparative purposes, 'dollars only' do not tell us a great deal because sales or revenue dollars vary. For example, the firm reduced operating expenses from $20 million in 2012 to $19 million in 2013. Good job? If sales in 2012 were $100 million, operating expenses were 20% of revenue. If sales in 2013 were $85 million, operating expenses were 22.4% of sales. This certainly suggests that management did not have spending under control during a period of declining revenue.

2. **Calculate the Key Financial Ratios**

   The most pertinent ratios will be described later this chapter.

3. **Evaluate the Firm's Trends Over Time**

   The internal financial analysis should evaluate the recent financial trends of the firm. I prefer to utilize three years history plus the current full year projection. Both common sized income statements and the key financial ratios should be analyzed.

4. **Compare and Analyze the Firm's Financials Against Competition and the Industry**

   This analysis should include comparing both the income statement and key ratios versus the top competitors, as well as market share, sales growth, and related trends. If the firm's primary competitors are privately held or are a business unit of a diversified corporation, published financial information is either limited or non-existent. In these instances, knowledge of competitor pricing, customer base, geography, capacity, etc. should yield close approximations of actual financial performance.

Unit Pricing and Margin

The simple formula for pricing and gross margin is ***Price Equals Cost Plus Gross Margin***. When pricing individual products, the basic formula to determine gross margin is:

Gross Margin % = (Price – Cost) / Price

For example, if the firm's selling price of product A is $30 and the standard cost is $20, then the gross margin percent is 33.3% ($30 - $20/$30). Using the same basic formula, if a firm's cost is $30 and gross margin is 40%, the selling price equals $50 ($30 / 0.6).

Market Share

Market share represents the firm's (or a competitor's) portion of total industry revenue. If the size of an industry is $400 million and the firm has revenue of $80 million, market share is 20% ($80/$400). Market share trends for the firm and their competitors are important to track over time. A word of caution should be noted. Even if the company is growing revenue, if the industry is growing more rapidly than the company, market share is being lost. Translation . . . the firm's strategy is not working and corrective action is warranted.

Percent Change from Prior Period

This is particularly important evaluation for both revenue and profits.

(Current Period $ / Prior Period $) – 1 = Percent Growth (or Decline)

For example, if this year's sales were $90 million and last year's sales were $80 million, the firm grew its sales by 12.5% (90 / 80 - 1). This allows managers to discern trends over time and represents an important calculation for the investment community. For retailers, changes in weekly and monthly revenues from the prior year is a frequent performance benchmark. Care must be taken, however, to ensure the comparison is apples-to-apples. For example, WalMart's stock recently dropped when there was a sales decline from current March to prior year March. Conversely, their stock jumped in April when comparison to prior year was very favorable. Why? The comparisons were invalid because prior year Easter was in March, and it was in April during the following year. This is noteworthy, as Easter represents one of the peak selling seasons for general merchandise.

The Common Sized Income Statement

Once the firm's and competitive income statement are common sized, many of the trend and comparative calculations have already been made, as outlined below.

Cost of goods sold as a percent of sales . . . how well the company is managing their COGS.

Gross margin as a percent of sales . . . percent of revenue available to cover operating expenses and yield a profit.

Operating expenses as a percent of sales . . . how well is the company managing operating expenses.

Operating profit as a percent of sales . . . profitability from regular operations; sometimes termed "return on sales."

Net profit as a percent of sales . . . bottom line profitability after interest and taxes.

Return on Assets

The return on assets calculation reveals the profit generated per dollar of assets employed.

Profit / Average Total Assets = ROA %

Either operating profit, net profit, or both can be used in the calculation. Total assets include both current and fixed assets. Average total assets are utilized to eliminate seasonal or other fluctuations, particularly inventory, that may yield faulty conclusions. Companies will often use the trailing twelve or thirteen months when computing. ROA can vary considerably from industry to industry, primarily attributable to capital assets required to maintain participation in the business.

Return on Equity

Profit / Total Equity = ROE%

If benefitting the shareholders and investors is the most import goal of the firm, then return on equity becomes one of the most critical measurements, as this defines how the shareholders and investors have fared. It is sometimes referred to as "return on net worth." For public firms, 12% - 15% is a typical ROE.

Inventory Turns

As discussed in Chapter 5, management of inventory is frequently a contributor to financial underperformance. Failure to recognize and devalue excess and obsolete inventory overstates financial performance until such time as the inventory is either sold off or destroyed.

Cost of Goods Sold / Average Inventory = Inventory Turns

365 Days / Inventory Turns = Days Supply in Inventory

The higher the number of inventory turns and/or the lower the days supply are favorable indicators. Average inventory, as indicated previously, is used to eliminate seasonal or other fluctuations.

Days Sales Outstanding (DSO)

The DSO calculation tells us how well accounts receivable are being managed . . . how fast we collect on the products and services sold to customers. Average receivables is utilized to eliminate seasonal or other short term fluctuations. The lower the days outstanding, the better the firm is managing accounts receivable. Like inventory, receivables can represent a significant portion of company current assets and is frequently mismanaged. Many firms term days sales outstanding as "average collection period."

Sales / Average Accounts Receivable = Receivables Turnover

365 Days / Receivables Turnover = DSO (days sales outstanding)

While somewhat beyond the scope of strategic analysis, DPO (days payable outstanding) is a valuable tool to evaluate how rapidly we pay our suppliers and vendors. The larger the DPO the better, as firms should strive to secure extended dating on their accounts payable. A simple question worth posing is "if our customers are paying us in 45 days, why the hell are we paying our suppliers in 30 days?" The rationale here is we should be paying our suppliers in no fewer days then our customers are paying us.

Consider the case of Costco Wholesale Clubs. Costco inventory turns their 4,000 SKU's (stock keeping units) twelve times per year, or every 30 days (360 days/12). However, they are paying their suppliers in an average of 45 days. Accordingly, Costco is running their company on their supplier's money! WalMart has achieved similar results. Obviously, these are enviable financial positions to achieve.

Solvency Measures

Current Ratio – Short Term Solvency:

Current Assets / Current Liabilities = Current Ratio

Typically, if the current ratio is less than 1.0, the firm is in jeopardy of not being able to meet their financial liabilities. A current ratio of 2.0 or higher is regarded as a strong indicator of solvency. For this calculation, current assets include cash, accounts receivable, and inventory. Many firms prefer the 'quick ratio', which is cash plus receivables divided by current liabilities. This factors out inventory and avoids a misleading evaluation in cases where there is excess and obsolete inventory that has not been devalued, thus inflating the current ratio.

Debt to Equity Ratio – Long Term Solvency:

Total Debt / Total Stockholders Equity = Debt to Equity Ratio

This describes the firm's long term ability to meet its financial obligations. If debt is greater than equity (ratio is less than 1.0), this indicates the firm has a weak balance sheet, excessive debt, and generally low credit worthiness.

Times Interest Earned – Long Term Solvency:

Operating Profit / Interest = Times Interest Earned

This calculation exhibits the firm's ability to pay the interest on its debt, which is particularly crucial to private equity investors, as operating profit after debt is used to pay down the debt itself. Most lenders require a minimum ratio of 2.0, with 3.0 being considered very healthy.

Market Value Measures

Market Capitalization:

Number of Shares Outstanding x Stock Price = Market Capitalization

The faulty logic of many novice investors and students is that a firm's stock price is a measure of the firm's value (i.e. a competitor with a stock price of $20 is more valuable than one with a stock price of $15). For comparative purposes, market capitalization yields the true comparative value of the firm. Only stock price movement over time is relevant.

Earnings Per Share / PE Ratio:

Net profit / Number of Shares Outstanding = Earnings per Share

Market Price per Share / Earnings per Share = Price – Earnings Ratio

The Price – Earnings Ratio, for publicly traded companies, quoted daily in the primary financial journals, has become somewhat an obsession of stock evaluators and traders. Competitors in different industries can have vastly different PE ratios, so care should be exercised in using this evaluation. Typically a PE ratio above 20 indicates a high level of investor confidence in the firm's outlook and earnings potential, whereas a PE ratio below 12 suggests either high risk or stagnant growth. While current PE ratios are typically published, projected future PE ratios would seem to be a more relevant analysis.

Given the very short-term focus firms and investors place on U.S. companies, I like to call this obsession *EPSPS . . . Earnings per Share per Second*. Company management is under constant pressure from investors and boards of directors to produce better than expected results each and every quarter. In many cases, executives are in jeopardy of losing their jobs and bonuses if quarterly performance does not meet expectations. This often results in decisions not in the best intermediate and long-term interest of the organization, yielding delays in needed investments, generation of unprofitable sales, failure to recognize obsolete inventories and incurred costs, etc. An analogy is our federal government and social security and failure to reserve against shortfalls until they come due. Politicians fear that they will not get reelected if major changes or benefit reductions are implemented. They will be retired when the shortfall hits, so it will be the next elected official's problem.

Consider the example of Toyota and Honda. They entered the U.S. market in the late 1970's and early 1980's, and did not make a profit until the early 1990's. Clearly, their investment in the U.S. market has paid significant long-term dividends. Would the investment community and boards of directors accept this long term investment to secure a market position by a United States automaker? Not likely.

Free Cash Flow

(Net Profit + Depreciation) – (Capital Expenditures + Dividends)

This represents an estimate of the cash the firm generates after payment of operating expenses, taxes, interest, dividends and reinvestments. The larger the free cash flow, the greater the ability to internally fund new strategic initiatives, repay debt, increase dividends, and/or repurchase stock shares.

Chapter 5
The Company (Internal) Environment

"Before management can chart a new strategy, they must reach

common understanding of the company's current position"

With an understanding of the key financial measurements and how they are calculated, we can now begin to evaluate the firm's performance over time and against competition. At this point, a word of caution is appropriate. Too many firms place too much emphasis on the firm's internal environment and capabilities at the exclusion of what's really important . . . satisfying customer needs. It took GM and Ford twenty years to respond to the Japanese strategy of simply giving consumers what they wanted, rather than what was convenient to manufacture. How well did Polaroid respond to the digital photography trend? How well did music and video stores respond to iTunes, streaming, and the success of Amazon? Management must also consider not only direct, but indirect and substitute competition. Brick and mortar retailers have certainly been impacted by internet retailing. Advances in video conferencing have adversely impacted business passenger airline travel. Why is Circuit City and Borders located in the graveyard? I am sure the reader can cite a number of additional examples.

Internal Financial Analysis

Exhibit 5 – 1 Acme Widget Company Abbreviated Financial Statements ($000,000)				
	2010	**2011**	**2012**	**2013**
Total Industry Widget Revenue	$500	$540	$580	$615
Income Statement				
Total Revenue	$100.0	$105.0	$110.0	$115.0
Sales Deductions	$5.0	$5.0	$5.0	$5.0
Net Revenue	$95.0	$100.0	$105.0	$110.0
Cost of Goods Sold	$60.0	$62.0	$64.0	$66.0
Gross Profit	$35.0	$38.0	$41.0	$44.0
Operating Expenses	$20.0	$21.5	$23.0	$24.5
Operating Profit	$15.0	$16.5	$18.0	$19.5
Interest and Taxes	$5.0	$5.5	$6.0	$6.5
Net Profit	$10.0	$11.0	$12.0	$13.0

Balance Sheet	2010	2011	2012	2013
Average Cash Balance	$5.0	$5.0	$5.0	$5.0
Average Receivables	$10.0	$10.5	$11.0	$11.5
Average Inventory	$12.0	$13.5	$14.8	$15.5
Total Average Current Assets	$27.0	$29.0	$30.8	$32.0
Average Fixed Assets	$35.0	$37.0	$38.0	$39.0
Total Average Assets	$62.0	$66.0	$68.8	$71.0
Current Liabilities	$20.0	$22.0	$23.0	$24.0
Long Term Debt	$20.0	$20.0	$20.0	$20.0
Total Liabilities	$40.0	$42.0	$43.0	$44.0
Shareholder Equity	$22.0	$24.0	$25.8	$27.0
Total Liabilities and Equity	$62.0	$66.0	$68.8	$71.0

The internal financial analysis simply evaluates the firm's financial performance and trends over time. **Exhibit 5 - 1** displays sample abbreviated financial statements for the Acme Widget Company. What does this statement tell us about the financial performance of the company? Actually, very little.

Exhibit 5 – 2
Acme Widget Company Financial Statement Trend Analysis ($000,000)

	2010	2011	2012	2013
Market Share	20.0%	19.4%	19.0%	18.7%
Common Sized Income Statement				
Total Revenue	100.0%	100.0%	100.0%	100.0%
% $ Change from Prior Year	6.7%	5.0%	4.8%	4.5%
Sales Deductions	5.0%	4.8%	4.5%	4.3%
Net Revenue	95.0%	95.2%	95.5%	95.7%
Cost of Goods Sold	60.0%	59.0%	58.2%	57.4%
Gross Profit	35.0%	36.2%	37.3%	38.3%
Operating Expenses	20.0%	20.5%	20.9%	21.3%
Operating Profit	15.0%	15.7%	16.4%	17.0%
Interest and Taxes	5.0%	5.2%	5.5%	5.7%
Net Profit	10.0%	10.5%	10.9%	11.3%
% $ Change from Prior Year	8.0%	10.0%	9.1%	8.3%
Performance Ratios	**2010**	**2011**	**2012**	**2013**
Net Profit Return on Assets	16.1%	16.7%	17.4%	18.3%
Return on Equity	45.5%	45.8%	46.5%	48.1%
Inventory Turns	5.0x	4.6x	4.3x	4.3x
Days Sales Outstanding	36.5 Days	36.5 Days	36.5 Days	36.5 Days
Current Ratio	1.4	1.3	1.3	1.3
Debt to Equity Ratio	0.91	0.83	0.78	0.74

Exhibit 5 – 2 common sizes the income statement and calculates the key financial ratios, as outlined in Chapter 4. Now, we can analyze how the Acme Widget Company is actually performing and evaluate both positive and negative trends

Favorable Trends:

- **Revenue Growth** . . . the company is growing revenue annually, however, at a decreasing rate. **Caution!** See Unfavorable Trends, as this sales growth is actually a company weakness!

- **Sales Deductions** . . . declining as a percent of revenue. Sales deductions include items such as cash discounts, customer accruals, returns, etc.

- **Cost of Goods Sold** . . . has decreased from 60% to 57.4% of revenue, suggesting that the firm is doing a good job of controlling costs and/or implementing cost reductions. A portion of this reduction is likely to be associated with economies of scale.

- **Operating Income / Net Income** . . . both are increasing as a percent of sales.

- **Return on Assets** . . . has grown from 16.1% to 18.3%.

- **Return on Equity** . . . shareholders are doing reasonably well, as ROE has been showing slight increases annually.

- **Debt to Equity Ratio** . . . while this ratio remains a concern, the company is able to meet its financial obligations and the ratio is improving.

Unfavorable Trends:

- **Market Share** . . . While the company's revenues are increasing, they are losing market share, as the industry is growing faster than the company, which indicates their present competitive strategy is not working. This must be addressed in their strategy.

- **Operating Expenses** . . . In most instances, operating expenses as a percent of higher revenue should decline due to better coverage of fixed expenses. Acme's expenses are increasing as a percent of revenue, suggesting that management must take a critical review of spending.

- **Interest and Taxes** . . . Also increasing as a percent of sales, indicating further review and understanding is needed.

- **Inventory Turns** . . . The decline in inventory turns from 5.0 times to 4.3 times (73 to 85 days supply) should be regarded as a major concern. Management needs to take immediate corrective action to reverse this trend.

- **Current Ratio** . . . While there has been a slight decline and the ratio remains over 1.0, a ratio of 1.3 is not a particularly strong indicator of solvency.

Areas of Potential Concern

In virtually every troubled company in which I have been associated, poor inventory management has been apparent. In all cases, excess and obsolete inventory was not identified and devalued. The cause is generally either management apathy in controlling inventory or overt disregard in devaluing inventory due to a resulting adverse effect on profitability.

On at least a semi-annual basis, I would have the IT Department run a simple inventory report on all products in the company's product line(s). This report would place each item in one of five inventory "buckets" as follows:

- 0 - 60 days supply . . . Good, as long as customer needs are being satisfied.
- 61 - 120 days supply . . . Fair, need to monitor to ensure there is no unnecessary build.
- 121 – 180 days supply . . . A potential pending problem; examine closely to determine if special promotion or other action is required.
- 181 – 360 days supply . . . crisis pending, investigation and action required now; begin devaluation if appropriate.
- Over one year supply . . . devalue inventory; establish liquidation plan.

Another frequent contributor to inventory issues is product proliferation. Many times, firms will introduce hundreds of new products annually, while failing to eliminate low volume or displaced products. One approach I have utilized is to have marketing personnel, on a semi-annual basis, prepare a tops down product-by-product sales report, in both unit volume and dollar volume. Marketing is then charged to either justify or discontinue/obsolete the bottom (lowest selling) 20% of products. Another approach is to require that, for every new product introduced, at least one product must be discontinued.

The following are a couple of personal examples of companies, for which I was given responsibility, where prior management mismanaged inventory, disguising the true operating condition of the organization.

Having become involved in early November, one of the company's product lines had three years supply of inventory, and the product being sold was at 25% under fully absorbed standard cost. Yet, the factory was running two shifts to produce more product. Why? Management bonuses were based on profitability, so the factory was running two shifts in order to generate greater burden absorption and thus, enhancing profitability. In addition, there was $3 million in inventory of another of the company's product lines sitting in a field in Alabama adjacent to a closed factory that remained fully valued. (I might add that there were creatures living inside of the product that were adverse to human presence.) We were fortunate to be able to sell this product at 8% of cost to a distributor in Eastern Europe, thereby only incurring a $2.75 million inventory loss. Payment of bonuses to the prior management was denied (as was their continued employment).

A second example is the condition of a firm owned by a private equity company. Within several months after becoming the company's CEO, the following irregularities were discovered:

- In many business environments, customers are offered financial incentives to drive greater purchase volumes. These year-end payments or rebates do not occur until after the close of books, which occurs in the next fiscal year. These are liabilities incurred in the prior year that must be reserved for in the year incurred. In this instance, there was almost $5 million in such incentive payments for which there were no reserves, thus reducing profitability by the full amount in the next year.

- The company's second and fifth largest customers were lost to competition in the last month of the fiscal year. This loss was not reflected in the following year forecast, thus significantly overstating revenues and profit.

- Once again, there was a proliferation of obsolete inventory for which a necessary $3.5 million in write-downs were required.

The result was nearly a 50% decline in the current year's profitability that had been provided to the firm's outside investors. Management of the private equity parent requested that, at the quarterly investors meeting, I mislead the investors on the true condition of the company. This opportunity was declined and my employment was terminated.

Are these types of activities illegal? Not really. Are they unethical and immoral? I certainly believe so. And, these are not unique accounts of financial mismanagement . . . activities such as this are more common than most readers would expect.

External Financial Analysis

As the title suggests, the external financial analysis compares the firm's financial performance against those of its leading competitors. As mentioned in Chapter 4, for public companies this is a fairly straight forward task. For privately held competitors, it requires a consolidation of the knowledge of competitors from the various functional areas of the company. *Morningstar.com* is the best information source I have found for public companies, as it provides all the common sizing and financial ratio calculations used in the external analysis.

Exhibit 5 - 3 displays the abbreviated financial statements of the Acme Widget Company and their three top competitors. Note that the total revenue for these four companies does not equal the industry total, as there are additional small competitors participating in the industry. For this exercise, only fiscal year 2013 is studied to avoid burdensome analysis. Similar to the internal financial analysis, **Exhibit 5 - 4** common sizes each company's income statement and calculates the key financial ratios, so that valid comparisons can be evaluated.

General Observations:

- **Competitor A** is the market leader and appears to be a well-managed organization and has minimal debt and a strong balance sheet. There appears to be only a couple areas of weakness versus Acme, as will be noted later. Competitor A should be the benchmark for Acme financial improvement.

Exhibit 5 – 3
Widget Industry Competitive Financials, 2013 ($000,000)

	Acme	Competitor A	Competitor B	Competitor C
Total Industry Widget Revenue	$615	$615	$615	$615
Income Statement				
Total Revenue	$115.0	$175.0	$120.0	$90.0
Sales Deductions	$5.0	$7.5	$7.0	$4.0
Net Revenue	$110.0	$167.5	$113.0	$86.0
Cost of Goods Sold	$66.0	$101.0	$75.0	$58.0
Gross Profit	$44.0	$66.5	$38.0	$28.0
Operating Expenses	$24.5	$31.5	$27.5	$23.0
Operating Profit	$19.5	$35.0	$10.5	$5.0
Interest and Taxes	$6.5	$12.0	$3.0	$3.0
Net Profit	$13.0	$23.0	$7.5	$2.0
Balance Sheet				
Average Cash Balance	$5.0	$19.0	$5.0	$1.0
Average Receivables	$11.5	$20.5	$15.0	$15.0
Average Inventory	$15.5	$19.5	$15.0	$15.0
Total Average Current Assets	$32.0	$60.0	$35.0	$31.0
Average Fixed Assets	$39.0	$40.0	$40.0	$35.0
Total Average Assets	$71.0	$100.0	$75.0	$66.0
Current Liabilities	$24.0	$30.0	$25.0	$20.0
Long Term Debt	$20.0	$10.0	$25.0	$25.0
Total Liabilities	$44.0	$40.0	$50.0	$45.0
Shareholder Equity	$27.0	$60.0	$25.0	$15.0
Total Liabilities and Equity	$71.0	$100.0	$75.0	$66.0

- **Competitor B** gained significant sales and market share growth versus 2012. It would appear, however, that this was achieved by "buying business" by reducing prices, which resulted in high cost of goods sold and operating expenses. The exception could have been investment and placement of new products, with high initial costs and marketing support.

- **Competitor C** is a troubled company, with declining sales and profits, high cost of goods sold and operating expenses, with nominal profitability, ROA and ROE. The balance sheet is weak. Acme should consider targeting this company for extinction and attacking their customer base. They could be an acquisition candidate if they have unique products or capabilities that would provide Acme with competitive advantages.

Favorable Acme Comparisons:

- Sales deductions appear well controlled.

- Favorable cost of goods sold . . . comparable to Competitor A and better than both B and C.

- Exceptional job of collecting receivables versus competition.

- ROA is solid, despite underperforming versus Competitor A. ROE is very favorable.

Exhibit 5 – 4
Widget Industry Financial Analysis, 2013 ($000,000)

	Acme	Competitor A	Competitor B	Competitor C
Market Share	18.7%	28.5%	19.5%	14.6%
Common Sized Income Statement				
Total Revenue	100.0%	100.0%	100.0%	100.0%
% $ Change from Prior Year	4.5%	6.1%	20.0%	-5.3%
Sales Deductions	4.3%	4.3%	5.8%	4.4%
Net Revenue	95.7%	95.7%	84.2%	95.6%
Cost of Goods Sold	57.4%	57.7%	62.5%	64.4%
Gross Profit	38.3%	38.0%	31.7%	31.2%
Operating Expenses	21.3%	18.0%	22.9%	25.6%
Operating Profit	17.0%	20.0%	8.8%	5.5%
Interest and Taxes	5.7%	6.9%	2.5%	3.3%
Net Profit	11.3%	13.1%	6.3%	2.2%
% $ Change from Prior Year	8.3%	6.5%	-11.1%	-55.0%
Performance Calculations				
Net Profit Return on Assets	18.3%	23.0%	10.0%	3.0%
Return on Equity	48.1%	38.3%	30.0%	13.3%
Inventory Turns	4.3x	5.2x	5.0x	3.9x
Days Sales Outstanding	36.5 Days	42.7 Days	45.6 Days	60.8 Days
Current Ratio	1.3	2.0	1.4	1.6
Debt to Equity Ratio	0.74	0.17	1.00	1.70

Unfavorable Acme Comparisons:

- Revenue growth is lagging behind the industry and competitors A and B. Thus, market share is being eroded.

- Operating expenses are increasing as a percent of sales and are significantly higher than those of Competitor A.

- Inventory management must be addressed as Acme is performing poorly versus both Competitors A and B.

- Current ratio is relatively weak, which is being driven by poor comparative inventory management.

- While the current debt to equity ratio is manageable, care should be taken to incur no additional long-term debt.

Sales Analysis

The next step in the analysis of the firm's internal environment is to review the following elements of the company's sales composition:

- Sales and profitability by channel of distribution

- Key customer sales and profitability

- Product sales mix; product and product line profitability

- Geographic sales, mix, and profitability

I have found many underperforming companies have failed to perform this fairly simple analysis. While no company or manager likes to lose revenue, this analysis often yields either necessary corrective action or, in some cases, abandonment of customers, channels, and/or products and product categories. In one instance, we found that we were serving a small distribution channel that was yielding significantly negative profitability. Rather than continue to directly serve a large number of small customers, we appointed geographic distributors to supply these customers. While we lost several million in revenues, the business we were able to retain generated favorable returns. In another instance, after finding that our 4th largest customer was producing a negative 10% operating income, and being unable to adjust pricing or program elements to rectify, we discontinued relations.

Frequently, companies will identify products or product categories that are yielding negative results. In some instances, it may be strategically necessary to continue to support, while in others the best course of action is to discontinue. It is not uncommon, when marketing to the big box retailers, to generate negative profit on opening price point (OPP) merchandise, which permits the retailer to hit advertising price points. If the overall customer is profitable and the OPP merchandise is crucial to protecting the firm's other placements, then the firm needs to accept the item loss. However, a valuable technique is to assign a broad functional representation of employees to brainstorm potential cost reductions on such products . . . I have seen some amazing results that have not compromised quality. The bottom line after completing the financial and sales analysis is:

Accordingly, the stronger the company's performance, the fewer strategic changes are needed.

Benchmarking and Best Practices

The management team who believes that "we do things better than anyone else" has their head in the sand and is ripe for competitive decline. Be assured, the 'invented here' syndrome is alive and well in many organizations, resulting in an unwillingness to change and improve.

Benchmarking is determining which companies, both within and outside the firm's industry, are best and most cost effective at performing various value chain activities. A Value Chain is defined as the various activities a company performs and how they compare to rivals. **Exhibit 5 - 5** displays a sample benchmarking for Acme Widgets versus their top three competitors.

Exhibit 5 - 5
Acme Widget Value Chain Comparisons

Value Chain Activity	Stronger than:	Same as:	Weaker than:
Costs (most important)	Co. B; Co. C	Co. A	
Pricing		Co. A; Co. C	Co. B
Financial Capabilities	Co. B; Co. C		Co. A
Management	Co. B; Co. C		Co. A
Marketing and Sales	Co. C	Co. B	Co. A
Operations/Production	Co. B; Co. C		Co. A
Distribution	Co. C		Co. A; Co. B
Procurement/Purchasing	Co. C	Co. A; Co. B	
Service		Co. A; Co. B	
Innovation	Co. C	Co. C	Co. A; Co. B

Where the firm is weaker than competition, corrective action should be considered. Where stronger than competition, the value chain element should be used to create competitive advantage and differentiation.

Management should also study firms outside its industry to determine who is best in the world at performing these activities. For example, Southwest Airlines average turn-around time, from arriving at the gate to departing from the gate, is 25 minutes. For the other major U.S. carriers, the turn-around time averages 50 minutes. Keep in mind, revenue is only being generated while the plane is in the air, not at the gate. Southwest certainly could not benchmark versus others in the industry. They studied and implemented the practices of who they believed had world class turn-around times . . . **NASCAR pit crews!**

Once the best practices are identified, the firm copies and implements these practices into their organization to improve the costs and effectiveness of their activities. Copying the success of others is not a sin, but it still requires management to admit someone else does it better.

What the company is seeking are elements of their marketing and competitive mix where sustainable competitive advantages can be identified and utilized. A sustainable competitive advantage must be valuable, rare, and difficult for others to copy or substitute for. In the early days of WalMart in the 1970's, their sustainable competitive advantage was location. Stores were placed in high traffic intersections in rural areas in the states surrounding Arkansas. At that time, their competition was located in or near major metropolitan areas. Today, I would propose WalMart's sustainable competitive advantage is twofold . . . low costs (as opposed to low prices) and their supply chain and logistics expertise.

A Word about Costs . . .

As you may have noted in **Exhibit 5 - 5**, "costs" was highlighted as the most important value chain element. There are three important factors to consider when it comes to costs:

1. The higher the company's costs above close rivals, the more competitively vulnerable it becomes.
2. The low cost global manufacturer and marketer may be the single strongest competitive advantage in most markets and industries.
3. Low cost DOES NOT necessarily mean LOW PRICE!

Exhibit 5 - 6 outlines several ways an organization can attack costs to enhance market position and/or improve profitability.

Prior to the beginning of each fiscal year, I would hold an annual off-site divisional management meeting to plan the coming year ahead. A critical element in this two to three day session was 'cost reduction brainstorming' . . . identifying ways we could eliminate costs and enhance profitability. After several hours, the group (about 20 managers) would generate over 100 costs/expense saving opportunities. We would then pick the top twenty ideas and each manager was assigned one cost reduction to captain and report on monthly. For theatrics, each manager signed in blood (i.e. red ink) that they would make their assigned cost reduction a reality. Not only did this approach yield positive results, it became an integral part of the company culture.

Exhibit 5 -6
Opportunities to Reduce Costs and Improvement Profitability

- Create a low cost company culture

- Relentless cost reduction and expense control efforts

- Benchmark and implement best practices

- Value engineer (study details of competitive product to determine cost saving opportunities)

- Top manager line-by-line budget reviews

- Reduce headcount

- Consolidate facilities

- Move manufacturing to lower cost areas (domestic or foreign)

- Redesign products

- Invest in cost and productivity improvements, including automation

- Pressure suppliers for better costs and terms; implement 'Just-in-Time' supplier inventories; regular supplier reviews and auctions

    BOTTOM LINE . . . Get rid of anything the customer is unwilling to pay for!

Chapter 6
The S.W.O.T. Analysis

Up to this point, our efforts have been acquiring and analyzing information. The SWOT (Strengths, Weaknesses, Opportunities, and Threats) Analysis consolidates the knowledge gained from understanding the general business environment, the market environment, the industry environment, the competitive environment, and the company's market and financial condition into manageable terms that will direct establishment of the strategic objectives.

STRENGTHS: What are the company's major strengths in the marketplace versus competition?

Strategy Implications: Leverage and utilize strengths as the strategic cornerstone.

WEAKNESSES: What are the company's major weaknesses in the marketplace versus competition?

Strategy Implications: Fix your competitive weaknesses.

OPPORTUNITIES: Where does the company have opportunities to grow the business and improve profitability, financial position, and stakeholder value?

Strategy Implications: Vigorously attack the company's opportunities.

THREATS: Where does the company have vulnerabilities and the potential to lose business and reduce profitability, financial condition, and stakeholder value?

Strategy Implications: Protect and defend against threats.

Management must conduct the SWOT analysis through the eyes of the firm's competitors, customers, and end users. All too often the internal company view is biased and tends to overstate the firm's strengths and understate the firm's weaknesses. Also, we must keep in mind that perception is reality. While we may be able to document and prove a strength, if the marketplace believes it to be a weakness, then it is not a strength. If you were to survey the general population regarding which automobile has better quality, Buick or Honda, 80-90% of the public would likely vote Honda. While empirical owner surveys and auto publication tests conclude Buick has superior quality, if prospective buyers are unaware or do not believe it to be a strength, then buyer perception wins. The company strategy, therefore, needs to address and correct erroneous perceptions.

Exhibits 6 - 1, 6 - 2, 6 - 3, and **6 - 4** outline some common strengths, weaknesses, opportunities, and threats experienced by many organizations.

Exhibit 6 - 1
Common Competitive Strengths

#1 = Low Cost Supplier

• Pricing	• Quality
• Financial Condition	• Innovation/New Products or Services
• Brand Equity; Preference	• Management/Organization
• Product/Service Differentiation	• Customer Service
• Broad Customer Base/Distribution	• Global Presence
• Economies of Scale	• Intellectual Capital
• Selection; Breadth of Line	• Technology
• Supply Chain Capabilities	• Manufacturing Efficiency

Exhibit 6 - 2
Common Competitive Weaknesses

• Cost Disadvantage (most important)	• Lack of Innovation/New Products
• Price Competitiveness	• Lack of Differentiation
• Financial Issues	• Management/Organization
• No/Limited Brand Equity	• Economies of Scale
• Limited Distribution	• Quality
• Minor or Declining Market Share	• Customer Service Issues
• Narrow Product/Service Offering	• Behind Technology Curve

Exhibit 6 - 3
Common Competitive Opportunities

• Cost Reduction; Expense Control	• New Valuable Features
• Price Leadership (if cost advantage)	• Quality Enhancements
• Differentiation	• New Technology Applications
• New Customers (specific)	• Attack Vulnerable Competitors
• New Distribution Channels	• Alliances/Joint Ventures
• Geographic Expansion	• Acquisitions
• New Products; Line Extensions	• Patents; Proprietary Assets
• Price Increases	• Facilities Consolidation/Relocation

Exhibit 6 - 4
Common Competitive Threats

• Increased or New Competition	• Change in Buyer Requirements
• New/Substitute Products or Services	• Price Erosion
• Declining Market Growth	• Catastrophic Events
• Competitor Consolidation	• Loss of Key Personnel
• Adverse Economic/Environment Conditions	• Increase in Buyer Bargaining Power
• Cost of Inputs/Materials	• New Government/Legal Requirements
• New Technologies	• Customer Financial Failures

Please note, in most industries, being the low cost domestic or global supplier is frequently the single most important strength a company can possess. Low cost DOES NOT mean just low standard cost. It must include all costs of the business model . . . marketing, distribution, administration, etc.

As an aid to developing the SWOT analysis, it can be meaningful to prepare what is termed a Competitive Strength Matrix. In Chapter 3, the Key Success Factors (KSFs) of an industry were developed. The Competitive Strength Matrix takes these factors, identifies the importance weights, and rates each of the major competitors (10 = favorable; 1 = unfavorable) on each factor. A weighted average for each competitor in then calculated. **Exhibit 6 - 5** attempts to present a Competitive Strength Matrix for the U.S. domestic automobile industry, keeping in mind that the factors and ratings are highly subjective and represent the opinions of the author.

Exhibit 6 - 5
Competitive Strength Matrix - U.S. Domestic Automobile Industry

Factor	Weight	Ford	GM	Chrysler	Toyota	Honda	Hyundai
Comparable Product Price	15%	7	6	8	7	7	9
Image/Perception	15%	6	5	3	9	8	4
Technology/Innovation	10%	6	5	3	8	8	6
Appearance/Styling	10%	6	6	7	8	8	7
Resale Value	10%	5	4	2	8	7	4
Comfort/Ride	10%	6	6	4	8	7	6
Operating Costs	10%	7	7	4	8	9	7
Product Selection	10%	7	9	8	6	5	4
Service/Warranty	10%	7	7	7	5	5	8
Weighted Average		**6.35**	**6.05**	**5.15**	**7.50**	**7.15**	**6.15**

In addition to providing guidance for the preparation of the SWOT analysis, there is an important lesson worth mentioning. If your company is Ford, based on this analysis, who should you attack first to produce the most immediate results? It is NOT Toyota or Honda! In all but a few select instances . . .

Firms should attack weakness rather than strength.

In the case of the domestic automobile industry, Ford's first line of attack should be Chrysler, the weakest competitor. A prudent rule of thumb is to attack the strongest competitors only when a significant vulnerability exists. As an example, several years ago when Toyota made headlines due to serious and dangerous quality issues, Ford successfully secured market share from Toyota by exploiting the quality issue and unfavorable publicity with a major safety and promotion program.

Immediate Action Requirements

Before moving forward with the preparation of the company strategy and key strategic objectives, management should first ask the question:

Does management have to take any actions, right now, to eliminate

dangerous weaknesses or threats?

In other words, do we need to table our strategy preparation and assign all of our resources to fix a major issue TODAY (or there may not be a tomorrow). In the aforementioned example, Toyota management, during the height of the quality and safety crisis, committed their resources to solving the crisis, not on their strategic imperatives one, two, or three or more years into the future. When it was discovered that select Mattel toys, manufactured in China, contained potentially harmful lead paint, management was focused on damage control and repair, not their future strategy.

Chapter 7
Generic Competitive Strategies

The basic generic strategies are the ways to kick the ass of rival companies

by doing a better job of satisfying buyer needs and preferences.

The majority of companies either participate in the broad marketplace, selling to the universe of potential buyers, or a niche (focused) market, selling to only a portion of the broad market and where buyers have specific needs or expectations. Toyota and their associated brands certainly are marketing to the broad market of potential automobile buyers. Conversely, Porsche markets to a very specific niche market of upscale sports car buyers with significant financial resources.

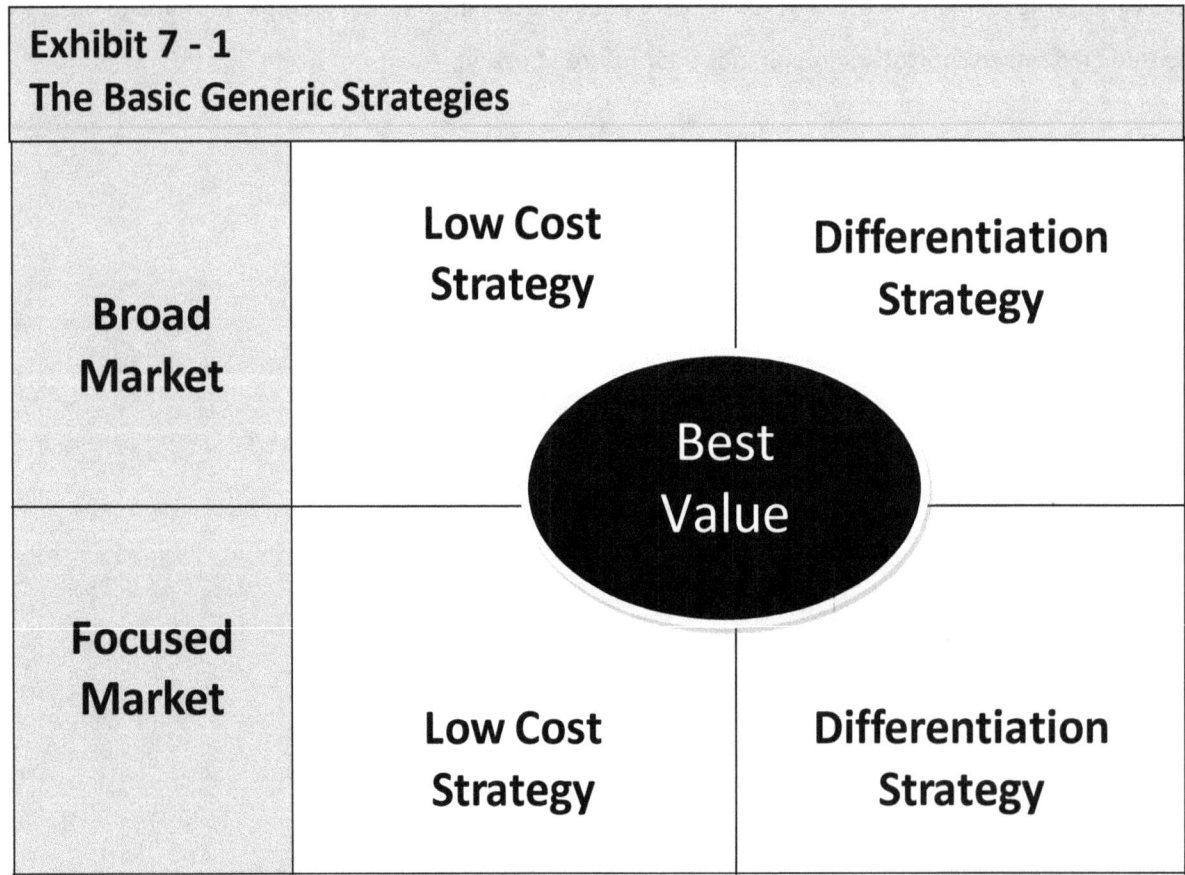

Exhibit 7 - 1
The Basic Generic Strategies

Broad Market	**Low Cost Strategy**	**Differentiation Strategy**
Focused Market	**Low Cost Strategy**	**Differentiation Strategy**

Best Value

As shown in **Exhibit 7 - 1**, whether participating in a broad market or a focused niche market, firms can choose one of three distinct strategic approaches . . . a **Low Cost Strategy**, a **Differentiation Strategy**, or a **Best Value** (combination of low cost and differentiation) **Strategy**. The following will review each of these three strategic approaches.

Low Cost Strategy

A **low cost provider strategy** makes achievement of lower costs than rivals the primary theme of the firm's strategy. However, features and services that buyers consider essential must be included in the product or service offering.   The most cost sensitive end user will not purchase a bad product, or a product or service that does not satisfy basic expectations.   In addition, management must find approaches to achieve a cost advantage in ways difficult for rivals to copy or match. As previously stated, low cost leadership means low overall costs, not just low manufacturing or production costs. And**, low cost does not necessarily mean low price**. Southwest Airlines has achieved lower operating costs than their competitors, but they are not always the lowest price alternative.

A low cost strategy generally works best under the following market conditions:

- Buyers are highly price sensitive
- Price competition is vigorous
- Product is standard or readily available from many suppliers
- There are few ways to achieve meaningful differentiation
- Buyer switching costs to change suppliers is minimal
- There are large buyers with significant power
- The economy is weak

What enticed WalMart to enter the grocery business? If you look at these market characteristics, most apply to the grocery/supermarket industry. WalMart is now the world's largest grocer.

There are essentially two ways to translate lower than competitive costs into greater profitability:

Option 1:   Use the low cost advantage to underprice competitors and attract price-sensitive buyers in enough numbers to increase total profits.

Option 2:   DO NOTHING. Maintain current pricing strategy, be content with volumes and market share, and use the lower cost advantage to earn higher profit margins and total profits.

Exhibit 7 - 2 compares these two alternatives. The firm has reduced their cost from $7.00 to $6.50 on an item which sells for $10.00 and generates 100,000 unit sales annually. The resulting gross profit is $300,000. If the price is reduced to $9.00, the firm must generate 120,000 unit sales to produce the same $300,000 in profit. However, if the firm does nothing and holds their price at $10.00, the result is $350,000 in gross profit. With the price reduction to $9.00, the firm must generate unit sales of 140,000 to produce the same $350,000 gross profit. Breakeven unit volume is even higher if investments must be made to generate the cost reduction. Accordingly, in many cases, doing nothing is a viable strategic option.

Exhibit 7 - 2
Cost Reduction Options to Increase Profitability

	Current	Reduce Price to $9.00	Do Nothing
Units	100,000	100,000	100,000
Price	$10.00	$9.00	$10.00
Cost	$7.00	$6.50	$6.50
Gross Profit	$300,000	$250,000	$350,000
Break Even Units to Generate $300,000		120,000	
Break Even Units to Generate $350,000		140,000	

Exhibit 7 - 3
Keys to Driving Down Costs

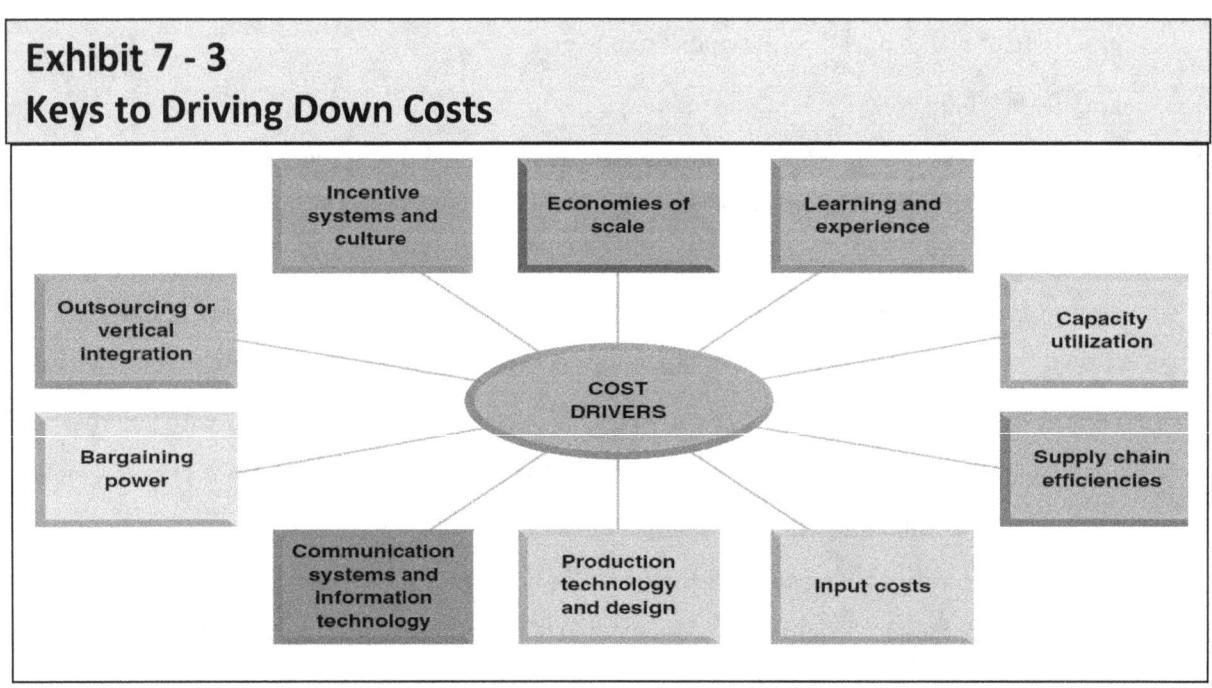

While discussed in earlier chapters, **Exhibit 7 - 3** displays the various ways a company can drive down costs to secure a competitive advantage.

Southwest Airlines is an excellent example of how a company can become a low cost provider. The following are several of their strategic elements in achieving low costs:

- 25 vs. 50 minutes at gate (no revenue is generated sitting at the gate!)
- Low cost, less competitive routes and cities . . . Lower landing fees
- Hedged oil prices
- No meals
- No assigned seating
- Same aircraft (service, parts, etc.)
- E ticketing . . . over 80% on-line vs. agents
- No baggage handling with other airlines
- No external third party web site costs
- Exceptional people with positive attitudes (this costs nothing)

There are, however, several potential pitfalls in developing a low cost strategy.

- Fixating on reducing costs and ignoring necessary features, quality and/or performance.
- Being overly aggressive in price cutting thereby reducing total profits.
- Implementing low cost methods that are easily imitated by rivals.
- Assuming competitors won't react to price reductions or program changes.

One of the most significant mistakes management can and does make is assuming competitors will not react. If, in the foregoing example, you reduce your product price from $10 to $9, competition is not going to sit idle and allow you to erode their market share. Management MUST consider potential competitive responses if pricing or other program elements are changed.

The growth of private label (i.e. house) brands continues to grow, particularly during periods of economic distress. Private label brands, like Great Value at WalMart, Archer Farms at Target, and Kirkland Signature at Costco hit significantly lower price points than national brands. According to a number of studies by _Consumer Reports_, the quality of private label merchandise is frequently equivalent to national brands. While European consumers tend to be more quality conscious than those in the United States, private label brands represent an even larger portion of consumer product sales in Europe as compared to the United States.

In many cases, breakthrough new product pricing tends to begin at very high levels, but, over time, can become commoditized and highly price competitive. At introduction, a 42" flat screen HD television sold for about $2,000. Today, the same set is frequently on sale for about $300. I purchased my first electronic calculator at Target in 1974 for $49.99 . . . the same calculator today is $1.99!

Computers and computer accessories have followed a similar pattern over the past decade. Management must take heed that the profit euphoria when product is in the early adaption stage may be rapidly eroded as new competition enters the market.

A Word About Low Cost Direct Importation

As we are all aware, many, if not most, manufacturers and retailers are sourcing products offshore in order to attain lower costs, with China and Pacific Basin countries being the primary sources. Many manufacturers have jumped on the China and others bandwagon because that is what their competition has done, without a comprehensive study of the real cost of Asian importation. United States manufacturers must consider retaining domestic production facilities through automation and other cost reduction efforts. In many cases, rather than going to the Pacific Basin, Mexico, Central America, or other 'local' countries should also be considered. The savings in freight, lower inventory requirements due to faster turn-around times (vs. 30 days transit from Asia), and travel can offset lower quoted costs. This has become even more significant as the value of the Chinese Yuan (RMB) has continued to strengthen and the cost of freight escalates.

Virtually all of the big box retailers have bypassed United States companies and are direct importing product directly overseas. It is estimated that over 10% of Chinese product entering the United States can be found on the shelves of WalMart! We were able to negate this process with WalMart and several others by preparing a financially sound analysis of the true costs associated with direct importation versus purchasing from domestic sources.

Exhibit 7 - 4 The Hidden Costs of Direct Importation	
How Does $1.00 Equal $.70?	
• Ocean Freight	• Travel Requirements
• Inland Freight	• Turn Around Time (2 vs. 30-60 days)
• Duty/Tariff	• Back Up Inventory
• Insurance	• Warehousing Costs
• Logistics Management	• Defectives and Returns
• Customs Clearance (foreign and domestic)	• On-Site Quality Inspection
• Letter of Credit; Other Transaction Costs	• Point-of-Sale Merchandising
• Terms; Cash/Early Pay Discounts	• Store Service
• Year End, Other Volume Incentives	• Advertising Funds; Ad Materials

Exhibit 7 - 4 outlines the various hidden costs associated with direct importation. We were able to convince several retailers, by assigning actual dollars to each of the hidden costs, that a $1.00 cost from a domestic marketer was equivalent to a direct F.O.B. China cost of about $.70. In other words, if we sold product to the retailer for $10.00, and the direct from China cost was more than $7.00, the retailer should purchase from the domestic source.

Differentiation Strategy

As the name implies, a successful **differentiation strategy** represents offering a product or service that has unique and appealing attributes that allow a firm to command a premium price, increase unit sales, increase profits, and/or build brand equity and loyalty, thus obtaining an advantage over competition. Often times, the inventor or innovator has what is termed a 'first mover advantage". But as previously noted, this advantage can be eroded over time as new competition enters the market and economies of scale are achieved.

Exhibit 7 - 5 displays the key competitive advantages companies utilize to sustain a strong differentiation strategy. These are regarded as the best choices to gain a longer-lasting, more profitable competitive edge.

Exhibit 7 - 5
Key Competitive Advantages to Sustain Differentiation

Differentiation Advantage	Examples
New Product Innovation	Apple; 3M; Golf Clubs; Mobile Communications; Computers/Software
Technical Superiority	IBM; Sony; Microsoft
Reliability	Toyota; Volvo (safety); Maytag
Quality	Karastan Carpets; Michelin Tires; Panera
Unique Features and Attributes	Dr. Pepper (23 flavors); Amazon One-Stop Shopping; Campbell's Soup Selection
Image	Ralph Lauren; Coach; Rolex; BMW; Mercedes Benz
Better Performance	Toyota Prius (gas mileage); John Deere; Southwest Airlines
Customer Service	Nordstroms; Federal Express; Ritz Carlton

As previously discussed, the perceived (intangible) differentiation can be just as or more important than actual (tangible) differentiation. Certainly designer clothing, select automobiles, upscale retailers, jewelry, perfume, etc. fall into this category.

There are a number of potential pitfalls of a differentiation strategy that management must guard against. If the difference or uniqueness is not valuable to the end user, differentiation will fail. In some cases, firms offer too much differentiation that confuses the potential end user. The price premium for the differentiating feature can be too great. In other instances, companies spend too much money on the differentiation . . . more than the end user is willing to pay, thus, eroding profitability.

Differentiation can fail if it can be easily imitated. In the early 1980s, American Airlines founded the 'frequent flyer program' in hopes of generating increased customer loyalty. The concept was a huge success, but American's major competitors were fast to follow, once they realized the program effectiveness. The result . . . airlines were giving away free flights that end users previously paid for, thus eroding both revenue and profitability of the entire industry.

If management is not cautious, brand image can be eroded through product line extensions that lower the value and perceived quality of their differentiated products. A classic example was Black and Decker's mid-1980s acquisition of General Electric's tabletop kitchen electrics and personal care appliances. Since the GE name could not be retained, management elected to put the B&D brand on these products. The result . . . B&D sales of professional power tools tanked. Why? Professional power tools are used predominantly by males on construction sites. Since there is a certain amount of macho involved, professional power tool users felt that "we're not going to purchase tools with the same damn brand as my wife's curling iron." The solution (after taking five years to identify the problem) was the acquisition of DeWalt, the leading professional power tool supplier. B&D rebranded their professional power tool line to the DeWalt brand and recovered much of their lost market share.

Assume for a moment that you are a Harley Davidson motor cycle owner. How would you feel if they introduced a new line of Harley Davidson motor scooters? No doubt their brand image and purchaser base would be eroded.

Best Value Strategy

A **Best Value Strategy** combines a strategic emphasis on low cost with a strategic emphasis on differentiation. The objective is to exceed buyer expectations in terms of attributes, performance, and price. It involves providing an upscale product or service at a lower cost and giving customer's better value for their money.

A recent study of 1,800 firms evidenced that firms who employed a best value strategy were more likely to outperform businesses that employed only a low cost or a differentiation strategy. And, it is more difficult for competitors to duplicate a best value strategy.

An example of a successful best value strategy is the Toyota Camry. Let's say a new Camry costs the end user $22,000, while a similar Chevrolet Malibu costs $20,000. Why do the majority of perspective buyers elect to purchase a Camry?

1. **Differentiation** . . . whether real or perceived, many consumers believe that the Camry offers important differentiating features such as better quality, safety, fuel efficiencies, ride, etc.

2. **Low Cost** . . . while currently Chevrolet is improving its resale value, after three years, the resale value of the Malibu was about 45% of the original purchase price, compared to 60% for the Camry. Accordingly, the resale value of the Malibu was about $9,000, compared to $13,200 for the Camry. The result is a $2,200 savings for the consumer after three years ($4,200 less the initial $2,000 higher purchase price).

The manufacturing cost of the Camry to Toyota is, in fact, lower than that of the Malibu due to a variety of factors, including lower legacy costs (i.e. retiree benefits), significantly lower union wages, parts commonality, and Toyota's lean manufacturing methods. In a service industry, Southwest Airlines is the leading U.S. passenger airline, in terms of number of domestic passengers, using a best value strategy combining an emphasis on low costs and differentiating features for potential passengers.

In the study previously cited, it was also found that firms who were "stuck in the middle" had the lowest overall performance. Stuck in the middle occurs when the low cost leaders begin siphoning customers away with a lower price, while differentiators seduce customers with better product or service attributes.

In the women's clothing business, the two most important factors in purchase decisions would seem to be low prices and fashion. A portion of the current struggles of J.C. Penney and Sears is an example of being stuck in the middle. The low cost providers (WalMart, Target, T.J. Max, etc.) continue to sustain low prices while offering greater and greater fashion. The high-end differentiators, on the other hand (department, specialty stores, factory stores), offer better fashion and frequent sales. The result has been the decline in revenue and profits for Penney and Sears, as they are getting squeezed smaller and smaller, having neither a cost advantage nor a differentiation (fashion) advantage. In addition, Kohl's has further eroded their business with a successful best value strategy.

Exploiting the Industry Profit Pool

A number of companies have successfully expanded their purviews to include both upstream and downstream expansion into related product and service categories. In the automotive business, manufacturers have extended their reach to include loans, leasing, rentals, insurance, ownership of dealers, etc., resulting in incremental revenues and profits.

U Haul represents an excellent example of exploiting the industry profit pool. Truck rentals is a competitive, low margin business, but U Haul has been successful in expanding their horizons to include other move-related goods and services . . . insurance, moving accessories, packing boxes, tape, protective blankets, packing materials, etc. These are all high margin add-ons that provided a needed service to consumers that could not be easily obtained elsewhere. U Haul has now even expanded into storage facilities at their truck rental locales.

WalMart has accomplished similar profit pool expansion by offering auto service, optical, check cashing, beauty shops, leased fast food chain departments, pharmacy, photo finishing, vendor kiosks, etc. All of these generate incremental revenue and profit for WalMart. And, if you are waiting for your auto to be serviced, what do you do? You shop for groceries and/or general merchandise.

Serving Niche and Focused Markets

The foregoing discussions related largely to the broad market for a firm's goods and services. Many smaller and mid-size organizations have been highly successful by concentrating their attention and strategies on a narrow piece of the overall market and avoid competing with the broad market leaders. Management needs to define and choose market niches where buyers have distinctive preferences, special requirements, or unique needs. The most common niches are those that involve more specialized products and service, such as Porsche (high performance sports cars), Sargento (cheese), Cannondale (high-end mountain bikes), TV stations (Animal Planet, Tennis Channel), and microbreweries and wineries. CGA Insurance services the unique market of amateur golf and charity tournament sponsors, ensuring against a hole-in-one, where high-end automobiles are frequently offered. A niche market can also be price point specific (Motel 6), geographic specific (Publix), end use specific (Enterprise auto rentals while cars is being repaired), etc.

Niche markets with the following characteristics can be attractive for focusing upon:

- Large enough to be profitable
- Appealing growth potential
- Not crucial to the success of the broad market leaders
- Costly or difficult for competitors to enter
- Company has resources and capabilities to effectively serve the market
- Few competitors are serving the niche

It should be noted that there is no correct or incorrect answer as to whether a company is participating in a broad or niche market. Take the case of Whole Foods. One could correctly argue that they participate in a niche market for organic and natural foods. Given their growing number of stores and the greater consumer focus on healthy eating, one could also build a case that they participate in the broad grocery market.

A focused low cost strategy attempts to serve the niche at a lower cost and price. Perrigo manufacturers and markets private label brand over-the-counter drugs for customers such as WalMart,

52

Walgreens, and grocery stores. Motel 6 appeals to truckers and interstate travelers. A number of online eyeglass suppliers have emerged, selling product at about one third versus optometrists.

A focused differentiation strategy attempts to serve buyers in the niche that have specialized preferences, needs, and/or applications. Haagen-Dazs ice cream, Godiva chocolates, and Gore cold weather fabrics are examples. Interestingly, Ferrari allocates only 1,500 automobiles annually for the United States and has over 20,000 registered buyers for their annual lottery. Many companies have been founded on servicing niche markets, but then expand to the broad market. Progressive Insurance, for example, began by providing auto insurance to high risk consumers, teenagers, high performance sports cars, and motorcycles. They now have successfully expanded into the broad market.

A focused best value strategy in niche markets also outperformed companies that utilize only a single lost cost or differentiation strategy. Buyers in the selected niche must be sensitive to both a value price and differentiated features. Lexus has become the number one worldwide marketer of luxury automobiles. In the United States, they have successfully implemented a best value strategy. They outperform Cadillac and Lincoln in terms of real and perceived features and quality. Lexus is considered in the same performance class with Mercedes and BMW, but at a lower price point. The result is that they are now number one in luxury automobiles in the United States.

There are several pitfalls to niche market strategies. A broad market competitor may elect to enter the niche market. Historically, Marriott hotels provided upscale accommodations near airports and in downtown locales. Over the past 20 years, they have expanded their purview to include luxury hotels (J.W. Marriott, Ritz Carlton), business traveler locations (Courtyard, Spring Hill Suites), long-term stay lodging (Residence Inns), and economy alternatives (Fairfield Inns). In addition, there is always a risk of new competitors entering the niche market, which can erode both cost and differentiation positions.

While on a consulting assignment in Orlando, Florida, I frequented a restaurant in a strip mall adjacent to a major traffic street. Within a six month period, four retail establishments in the mall went out of business . . . a bar stool store, a fireplace accessory store (in Florida?), a ceiling fan store, and a pleated blind store. Why? These retailers simply attempted to sell to a market niche that was too small to support these specialty establishments. Accordingly, niche marketers must ensure the niche market is large enough to support their business model.

Generic Strategies Recap

Exhibit 7 - 6 provides a general overview of low cost, differentiation and best value generic strategies. **Exhibit 7 - 7** displays a more detailed summarization of the strategic targets, basis of competing, product emphasis, production emphasis, and marketing emphasis of the generic strategies in both broad and niche markets.

Exhibit 7 - 6
Generic Strategies Recap

	Low Cost	Differentiation	Best Value
Strategic Basis	Lower costs than competition	Different from Competition	Better product, features; attractive price
Product Strategy	Low cost with acceptable quality	Different features or performance	Appealing features, quality at value price
Operations Strategy	Cost reduction and containment	Features buyers are willing to pay for	Better features, quality than competition at lower cost
Marketing Strategy	Promote low cost, equal performance	Valuable features not offered by competition	Better features and performance at competitive price

Exhibit 7 - 7
Generic Strategies Distinguishing Features

	Low-Cost Provider	Broad Differentiation	Focused Low-Cost Provider	Focused Differentiation	Best-Cost Provider
Strategic target	• A broad cross-section of the market.	• A broad cross-section of the market.	• A narrow market niche where buyer needs and preferences are distinctively different.	• A narrow market niche where buyer needs and preferences are distinctively different.	• Value-conscious buyers. • A middle market range.
Basis of competitive strategy	• Lower overall costs than competitors.	• Ability to offer buyers something attractively different from competitors' offerings.	• Lower overall cost than rivals in serving niche members.	• Attributes that appeal specifically to niche members.	• Ability to offer better goods at attractive prices.
Product line	• A good basic product with few frills (acceptable quality and limited selection).	• Many product variations, wide selection; emphasis on differentiating features.	• Features and attributes tailored to the tastes and requirements of niche members.	• Features and attributes tailored to the tastes and requirements of niche members.	• Items with appealing attributes; assorted features; better quality, not best.

	Low-Cost Provider	Broad Differentiation	Focused Low-Cost Provider	Focused Differentiation	Best-Cost Provider
Production emphasis	• A continuous search for cost reduction without sacrificing acceptable quality and essential features.	• Build in whatever differentiating features buyers are willing to pay for; strive for product superiority.	• A continuous search for cost reduction for products that meet basic needs of niche members.	• Small-scale production or custom-made products that match the tastes and requirements of niche members.	• Build in appealing features and better quality at lower cost than rivals.
Marketing emphasis	• Low prices, good value. • Try to make a virtue out of product features that lead to low cost.	• Tout differentiating features. • Charge a premium price to cover the extra costs of differentiating features.	• Communicate attractive features of a budget-priced product offering that fits niche buyers' expectations.	• Communicate how product offering does the best job of meeting niche buyers' expectations.	• Tout delivery of *best* value. • Either deliver comparable features at a lower price than rivals or else match rivals on prices and provide better features.

Chapter 8
Strategic Positioning

There are four parts to the very brief 'Strategic Positioning' section of the development of the business strategy:

- Generic Strategy
- Company Vision
- Company Mission Statement
- New Business Definition

Generic Strategy

As described in Chapter 7, it is recommended that management clarify their overall strategy. This should include whether the strategy is designed for the broad market or a focused/niche market and whether the positioning of the firm's strategy is as a low cost provider, a differentiation provider, or a best value provider. This declaration should establish a foundation for developing and implementing the firm's strategic objectives.

Company Strategic Vision

The company vision is the fundamental and enduring statement of management's long term aspirations for the business. The vision should be entrenched among both employees and stakeholders, as it provides a sense of direction for the firm's aggregate activities. A strong vision statement should be:

- Directional
- Inspiring and motivational
- Distinct
- Long-term oriented
- Passionate
- Easy to communicate
- Feasible (but not in the short term)
- **NOT** simply a public relations statement

Visions can backfire and fail if management does not walk the talk, as actions always trump words. They will also fail if they do not match the business and market environment or are unrealistic. In the classroom, I proposed a vision statement for Flagler College (2,600 students) to be:

"To become the largest college or university in the state of Florida."

Obviously, students find that to be a ridiculous vision. If the vision is not realistic, the dogs are simply not going to eat the dog food. Employees and stakeholders will not support it.

My two favorite visions are:

1. **"A car for every home"** (Henry Ford in 1908!)

2. **"Beat Xerox"** (Canon office products upon entering a market dominated by Xerox.)

Exhibit 8 - 1 communicates the vision statements of several well-known organizations. Some meet the criteria previously outlined, while others seem to miss the target.

Exhibit 8 - 1
Whose Vision Statements are These?

1. "To be the world's best quick service restaurant."

2. "To bring innovation and inspiration to every athlete in the world."

3. "To organize the world's information and make it universally accessible and useful."

4. "To satisfy the world's demand for fast, time-definite, and reliable distribution."

5. "To make London the safest major city in the world."

6. "Saving people money so they can live better."

7. "To help people improve the places where they live and work."

8. "Provide a global trading platform where practically anyone can trade practically anything."

1. McDonald's 2. Nike 3. Google   4. Federal Express 5. Scotland Yard 6. WalMart 7. Home Depot 8. eBay

---

Company Strategic Mission Statement

The company's mission statement essentially describes **"how we are going to accomplish our vision."** It is more specific than the vision and can change as the business environment and market conditions change. In one or two simple sentences, the mission statement of the company communicates:

- Purpose of the company

- Basis of competition and competitive advantages

- Focus on the means by which the company will compete

- How the company will satisfy customer needs

- The financial result

The following is an example mission statement of the Acme Widget Company:

"Over the next five years, achieve $400 million in revenue at 10% or greater

operating income through aggressive sales efforts, new products,

geographic expansion, rigorous cost and expense control, prudent asset

management, and superior customer service."

The actual mission statement for Federal Express is as follows:

"To produce superior financial returns for our shareholders

as we serve our customers with the highest quality transportation,

logistics, and e-commerce."

To recap, the company strategic vision states "where we are going," is enduring, and seldom changes. In contrast, the strategic mission statement communicates "how we are going to accomplish our vision," and it changes with the industry and market environment, responding to new threats and opportunities. And, don't forget K.I.S.S. (Keep It Simple Stupid). How do you communicate a four page vision or mission statement succinctly to employees and stakeholders?

The following example is the author's (not the company's) attempt at establishing the strategic positioning for the Ford Motor Company:

Strategic Position: Broad Market; Best Value

Vision: Leading the rebirth of the great American automobile.

Mission: Provide long-term value growth to our shareholders by expanding global market share through a combination of quality, efficient, environmentally sound, attractive, and competitively priced automotive vehicles and related products and services through prudent domestic and international investments.

New Business Definition:

In Chapter 2 - The Strategic Overview, we included the company's current business definition. Given the knowledge we have now acquired regarding the firm's opportunities and threats, should we change the business definition? In the case of the Acme Widget Company, let's assume the current definition states that they market their products in the United States and Canada. As a result of the analysis of the industry and competition, the company realizes that there is a significant opportunity to enter the Mexican and Central American markets. Accordingly, this should be included in the new business definition.

In Chapter 2, the suggested business definition for Southwest Airlines was:

"Southwest Airlines is a low cost North American passenger airline
offering superior customer service and value."

What if, as a result of the industry, market, and company analysis, Southwest decides to enter the 'local' international market and provide air freight services on their existing passenger routes and equipment? Southwest, therefore, should change its business definition to include this expansion. As a result, the new business definition would look something like the following:

"Southwest Airlines is a low cost passenger and airfreight airline that services

North America and select Mexico and Caribbean routes

with superior customer service and value."

The new business definition can be omitted if no changes are proposed.

Chapter 9
Strategic Objectives

Up to this point in the strategy preparation process, we have spent our energy in gathering and analyzing the firm's business environment, market and competitive environment, and the company environment. From this analysis, we developed the SWOT analysis for the firm. This SWOT analysis sets the stage for development and implementation of strategic objectives. At the risk of being repetitive, the strategic implications of the SWOT analysis were identified as follows:

STRENGTHS:	Leverage and utilize strengths as the strategic cornerstone.
WEAKNESSES:	Fix competitive weaknesses.
OPPORTUNITIES:	Vigorously attack the company's opportunities.
THREATS:	Protect and defend against threats.

Now, the rubber meets the road . . . specifying the objectives, action plans and related timetables. These are the organization's performance targets . . . the results and outcomes management wants to achieve. This is where the academic community comes up short and where students struggle; failure to connect the dots. In many cases, given the analysis and evaluations already performed, identifying the strategic objectives often becomes obvious.

Revenue and Profit Goals

Before establishing the strategic objectives, however, management should specify the revenue and profit targets they expect to achieve. Revenue objectives can either be in real dollars or percent growth, while profit objectives can be set in real dollars or as a percent of revenue. Net and/or operating profit can be utilized. Depending on the firm's key financial measurements, additional financial objectives may be included in the strategic objectives themselves. Typically, revenue and profit goals should be shown annually for a three to five year period forward, depending on the company's business model and planning horizon. The balance of the strategic objectives supports achievement of the revenue and profit targets. **Exhibit 9 -1** displays a sample revenue and profit goals matrix for the Acme Widget Company.

Strategic Objectives and Action Plans

The strategic objectives and related action plans are those things management must accomplish to achieve its revenue and profit goals, its mission, and drive toward realizing its vision. The strategic objectives are the organization's performance targets upon which management effectiveness must be evaluated. There are several key elements that must be addressed when establishing the firm's strategic objectives.

Exhibit 9 - 1
Revenue and Profit Goals, Acme Widget Company

	2013 Actual	2014 Goal	2015 Goal	2016 Goal
Revenue ($000,000)	$115.0	$122.5	$132.5	$140.0
Percent Increase from Prior	4.5%	6.5%	8.2%	5.7%
Net Income ($000,000)	$13.0	$15.0	$17.0	$18.5
Percent Increase from Prior	8.3%	15.4%	13.3%	8.8%
Percent to Revenue	11.3%	12.2%	12.8%	13.2%

- **A Balanced Scorecard**

    The concept of the balanced scorecard is fairly simple . . . a firm's strategic objectives should always be a combination of financial objectives and market-driven objectives. As discussed, in virtually all instances, firms must establish future revenue objectives and profitability objectives. **Exhibit 9 - 2** and **Exhibit 9 - 3** outline some typical supplemental financial and market-driven objectives, in addition to the revenue and profit goals established above.

Exhibit 9 – 2
Common Financial Objectives

- An X percent increase in annual revenues.
- Annual increase in after-tax profits of X percent.
- Annual increase of earning per share of X percent.
- Annual dividend increase of X percent.
- Profit margins of X percent or greater.
- Increase return on assets to X?
- X percent increase in return on shareholder equity.
- Secure bond and credit rating of X.
- Reduce operating expenses to less than X% of sales.
- Internal cash flow of $X to fund new investments.

Table 9 – 3
Common Market Driven Objectives
<ul><li>Secure X% market share.</li><li>Achieve lowest costs in industry.</li><li>Introduce X new products or product lines.</li><li>Offer wider product line than competition.</li><li>Secure X new customers.</li><li>Displace competitor X at customer Y.</li><li>Enhance brand image and recognition to X% and Y%.</li><li>Expand geographic distribution to include X.</li><li>Expand product lines to include X.</li><li>Secure minimum on time and complete customer service of X%.</li></ul>

- **Specific and Measurable**

  Improve customer service. Reduce operating expenses. Introduce new products. NONE of these are meaningful strategic objectives because they are neither specific nor measurable. As Bill Hewlett, founder of Hewlett-Packard stated "You cannot manage what you cannot measure and what is measured gets done." Strategic objectives must be specific so that both progress and outcomes can be monitored and evaluated.

- **Time-Defined**

  As with measurability, strategic objectives must be time-defined. If management does not specify when action must be undertaken and completed, it simply is not going to happen, as day-to-day activities will trump objectives that are not time defined. From the examples above, the following are specific, measureable, and time-defined objectives:

  - Improve and maintain customer on-time and complete shipping levels from 90% to 95% by year-end, 2014.
  - Reduce and maintain operating expenses from 20% to 18.5% of revenue in 2014.
  - Immediately begin development of new line of xxx products for introduction and availability by January 1, 2015.

- **Challenging (but achievable)**

  If a high jumper can clear seven feet, but the bar is never set to seven feet two inches, how does he know he cannot go higher if he never moves the bar? The same is true with strategic objectives. If the bar is set too low, once achieved, there is no motivation to strive for new heights. Objectives must be a stretch . . . challenging but realistic. If the bar is set unrealistically high, the organization can be de-motivated. Or, as we discovered within the past decade, management may take actions detrimental to the future of the organization or engage in illegal or immoral courses of action to achieve such objectives and maximize performance bonuses.

- **Short-Term and Long-Term Objectives**

  A combination of short-term and long-term objectives are needed. Too many companies have concentrated solely on short-term financial objectives, potentially dooming the long-term viability of the organization. Private equity firms and venture capitalists continue to be criticized for their short-term focus.

  What is short term and what is long term? It can be very different from industry to industry and company to company. If you are a high fashion clothier, your current planning horizon is likely to be nine to twelve months to deliver new seasonal selections. Pharmaceutical companies, on the other hand, have planning horizons seven to eight years into the future, as development, testing, and government approval of new drugs is a lengthy process.

- **Basis for Rewards and Incentives**

  If the revenue and profit goals and the supporting strategic objectives are the most important elements of an organization's success, **performance bonuses must be based on achievement of these goals and objectives**. Compensation plans for functional areas and individuals within those functional areas must directly relate to this achievement. As will be noted later in this guide, bonuses must extend beyond just top and key management to those individuals who ultimately must execute action plans. "I want you to work your ass off next year so I can maximize my bonus and buy my spouse a new Mercedes" does nothing to drive and motivate employees to achieve the most important goals and objectives.

- **Manageable Number of Objectives**

  Generally speaking, six to eight and no more than ten strategic objectives should be established. If a company sets twenty to thirty objectives management loses their ability to communicate, manage, and prioritize their activities.

- **Consistency**

   Unless there are dramatic changes in the marketplace, strategic objectives are frequently consistent from period to period without significant alteration. Take, for example, the U.S. Constitution. In the past 225 years since inception, there have only been a handful of changes to the original amendments. **Exhibit 9 - 4** cites the original objectives established by Starbucks. They certainly appear to have been successful in achieving their objectives, with many still an integral part of their ongoing strategy.

Exhibit 9 - 4
Starbuck's Original Strategic Objectives

- **Expand the number of domestic outlets.**
- **Make Starbucks a global brand.**
- **Create superior store ambience.**
- **Broaden in-store product offering.**
- **Grow out of store sales.**
- **Be socially and environmentally responsible.**
- **Control new store costs.**
- **Ensure customer friendly service.**
- **Starbucks must be a great place to work.**

- **COMMUNICATE!**

   The company's overall vision, mission, goals, and strategic objectives should be communicated at virtually all levels of the organization. If we have the organization community understanding and shooting at the same targets, the probability of success increases substantially. However, in some cases, careful editing may be necessary. For example, if one of the strategic objectives is to close an existing facility, this is not an objective that should be shared outside of only a handful of senior managers. Note . . . for companies with over fifty employees, management must provide a minimum of sixty days notification prior to facility physical closure.
Exhibit 9 - 5 displays the sample strategic objectives for the Acme Widget Company. Keep in mind that These objectives correspond to the revenue and profit goals established in Exhibit 9 – 1.

Exhibit 9 - 5
Acme Widget Company Additional Strategic Objectives

OBJECTIVE:	**Increase market share from current 18.7% to 21.5% by 2016, based on projected 2016 industry revenue of $650 million.**
Action Plan:	Acquire two major new customers ($1 million plus annually); 2014 emphasis on competitor B (quality and delivery issues).
	See additional objectives that follow.
OBJECTIVE:	**Increase return on assets from 18.3% to 25% by 2016.**
Action Plan:	Improve inventory turns to 5.0x or better (as major competitors have done).
	Reduce DSO from 36.5 to 32.5 days or less.
	Establish Just-in-Time inventory program with top 15 suppliers.
OBJECTIVE:	**Establish and achieve new cost and expense control parameters . . . NOW.**
Action Plan:	Reduce operating expenses to 20% of revenue or less.
	Reduce COGS 0.5% annually.
	Secure annual price increases compatible with the PPI and CPI.
OBJECTIVE:	**Develop and introduce a new line of digital residential widgets.**
Action Plan:	Good-better-best line ranging in price from $15 to $30 at retail.
	Complete market research immediately; complete development by January 1, 2015; customer availability April 1, 2015.
	Revenue goal of $5.0 million in 2015; $8.0 million in 2016.
OBJECTIVE:	**Close Michigan manufacturing facility by October 1, 2014.**
Action Plan:	Move high automation production to Kentucky facility.
	Move high labor content production to China joint venture.
	Advise impacted employees June 1, 2014; offer select stay bonuses to ensure production continuity through closure.
OBJECTIVE:	**Expand Distribution to Mexico.**
Action Plan:	Recruit three to five exclusive regional distributors; appoint internal employee to manage and train appointed distributors and their sales organizations.
	Appoint new manager by March 1, 2014; assign distributors by August 1, 2014.
	$2.0 million goal 2015; $3.5 million in 2016.
OBJECTIVE:	**Attempt to acquire XYZ Widget Company.**
Action Plan:	Annual sales of $10 million of which 75% would be incremental to Acme.
	Begin negotiations April 1, 2014; $4 million maximum purchase price, including debt obligations.
	If acquired, immediately consolidate for scale economies and remove redundant activities.
	Resulting sales and profits are not included in revenue and profit goals.
OBJECTIVE:	**Discontinue the Widget One product line.**
Action Plan:	Begin phase-out July 1, 2014.
	Sell any remaining inventory by January 1, 2015 at standard cost or greater.
	$3.5 million current annual revenue and declining; no profitability.

The job of crafting the strategy is actually the easy part. Now, the same management team who developed the strategy must gain support of the organization and execute the strategy. A weak strategy perfectly executed will beat a strong strategy poorly executed every time. This issue will be addressed in greater detail in future chapters.

Strategies Must Be Dynamic

The rate of change and uncertainty in today's business environment requires a constant assessment of strategic direction. We all now operate in a global environment with global manufacturers and service providers. Markets are changing, regional trade agreements have changed the global business landscape, currency exchange rates can make or break business activities, new competitors are entering markets at a rapid pace, while others are exiting markets, cultures are becoming more globalized, and political, legal, and social issues make global business complex. In today's world, we conduct business 24 hours per day, seven days per week.

Technology further forces strategies to be dynamic and ever changing. Companies who are behind the technology curve run the risk of becoming the infamous buggy whip. When I began my career, there were no computers, mobile phones, MP3s, satellite radio (there was no FM radio!), ATMs, cable TV (there were four networks only . . . ABC, NBC, CBS, and PBS), internet, email, or voice mail. I purchased my first electronic calculator in 1974 for $49.99 (the same one is at WalMart for $1.99). How many of you remember the slide rule? Have used a manual typewriter? Have carbon paper in your desk? The U.S. Postal Service, Borders, Blackberry, Nokia, Blockbuster, FM radio stations, and music stores are just a few of a plethora of examples of companies who have failed to respond to changes in technology and market composition.

Objectives Cascade

Strategic goals and objectives must cascade . . . top-down driven, not bottom up. In a multi business unit environment, corporate objectives must be first developed and communicated. Only then, can individual business unit objectives be established. These business unit objectives filter down to more specific functional area objectives within the business unit and ultimately to the individual contributors.

Corporate Objectives
▼
Business Unit Objectives
▼
Functional Area Objectives
▼
Individual Objectives

Certainly General Electric, with nearly $200 billion in sales and over a hundred diverse divisions ranging from financial services to aircraft engines to TV broadcasting to home appliances, is an example. Corporate management must rely on local business unit strategies under the umbrella of the overall corporate strategy. It is beyond the capabilities of corporate executives to understand the industry and market environment and intimacies of such diverse operating entities.

Corporate Governance and Strategy

Most would agree that the overall purpose of a corporation is to maximize the **long term return to the owners** (shareholders and stakeholders). I believe Asian businesses continue to outperform many U.S. corporations because they are much more willing to invest in the long-term viability of the firm, per the previously cited example of Toyota's and Honda's long range investment in the U.S. automotive market. So many U.S. organizations focus on what I term EPSPS . . . **Earnings per Share per Second**. Wall Street, shareholders, and boards of directors are forcing businesses to focus on short-term results . . . quarter to quarter if not month to month performance. In many instances, this drives decisions not in the best intermediate and longer-term viability of the corporation.

The role of the Board of Directors should be to:

- Ensure objectives align with shareholder and stakeholder interest.
- Validate the firm's business strategy.
- Ensure strong senior leadership.
- Implement compensation plans that serve shareholder interest.
- Ensure GAAP adherence.
- Drive ethical conduct and corporate citizenship.

There are certainly numerous examples where boards have failed to fulfill these obligations. I continue to be skeptical about corporations where the CEO and Chairman is the same person, resulting in an absence of checks and balances.

Compensation plans that serve shareholder interest are a particular concern. Boards must take responsibility and ensure key executives are **paid based on performance**. Recently, a major U.S. company terminated their CEO after five years on the job. During that period, I held the company's stock, which was ultimately sold for a small loss. However, the fired CEO received a severance package in excess of $200 million. Is that serving the shareholders best interest? I think not. Stockholder groups are now demanding greater board of director accountability and are pressing for increased oversight. Current public opinion of corporate leadership is disturbing:

- 90% believe corporations are not looking out for the best interest of their employees.
- 57% believe corporate executives are only are only in it for themselves.
- 82% state corporate executives are not looking out for the interest of shareholders.

And, this is not just an issue in the United States. Similar public opinions are evidenced in Europe, Australia, Canada, and other locales.

Consideration in developing strategies must be given, not only to shareholders and owners, but to employees, suppliers, customers, end users, and the communities in which operations are present. There is substantial evidence in today's environment that **GREEN = GREEN**. Those companies that have "green" elements in their strategies are outperforming those companies that do not, thus generating greenbacks. While there are a variety of definitions of "green," I consider there are three elements that must be addressed in a green strategy:

1. Environmentally Conscious
2. Socially Responsible
3. Ethical Behavior

A Final Word

We must not forget that a successful business strategy must contain two essential elements:

1. **The strategy must improve the company's financial strength and profitability.**

2. **The strategy must improve the company's competitive strength and market position.**

Chapter 10
Supplemental Strategies

In this chapter, we will present six strategy supplements . . . strategic compliments to support the chosen generic business strategy.

- Alliances and Partnerships

- Mergers and Acquisitions

- Vertical Integration versus Outsourcing

- Offensive and Defensive Strategies

- Internet Strategies

- Market Condition Strategies

Alliances and Partnerships

These are collaborative arrangements where two or more companies join forces, which may or may not be contractual, to achieve **mutually beneficial outcomes**. This includes joint ventures, which are alliances where the partners establish a jointly controlled separate entity. Today, an estimated 50% of U.S. corporations have formed strategic alliances, compared to only about 15% in 1995. Samsung, for example, is reported to have over 1,300 such alliances.

Strategic alliances are formed for a variety of reasons, including entry into international markets, access to new markets, to gain technological expertise, for scale economies, for manufacturing and service, and access to new distribution channels. Virtually all major U.S. manufacturing companies have formed alliances in the Pacific Basin, most frequently in China.

Approximately one out of every two strategic alliances are terminated within the first five years after establishment. The primary cause of divorce is the absence of mutual benefits, which will result in a divergence of partner objectives and priorities. In other cases, the partners are unable to play together in the sandbox. The former Northwest Airlines and the Dutch passenger airline KLM formed a strategic alliance that was eventually dissolved because the respective CEOs got mad at each other and refused to even talk.

Another danger is the "minnow bites the shark," where a company puts a partner in the business, the partnership dissolves, and the partner becomes a competitor. We formed a manufacturing alliance with a small Chinese firm that we discontinued due to quality and delivery issues. What did the Chinese manufacturer do? They went straight to our major customers and attempted to sell them direct at a considerably lower cost.

Mergers and Acquisitions

Mergers are a combination and pooling of companies of fairly equal size, with the newly created firm frequently taking on a new name. Examples of major mergers include HP and Compaq in computers, Kmart and Sears in retailing, Sprint and Nextel in communications, and Delta and Northwest Airlines. **Acquisitions** are when one firm, the acquirer, purchases and absorbs operations of another firm, the acquired. In the past decade there have been over 100,000 acquisitions in just the U.S., in addition to numerous foreign company acquisitions of U.S. companies while the United States dollar was weak.

Typical objectives for making mergers and acquisitions include:

- **Cost Efficiencies:** The most common objective is to secure economies of scale, making 2+2=3 in terms of costs by reducing personnel, consolidating procurement, administration, sales, marketing, etc., removal of redundant activities, and facility closures. For example, when Delta and Northwest Airlines merged, management estimated $1 billion in annual cost savings once consolidation was completed.

- **Market Power:** This relates to becoming more important in the marketplace with distribution channels, customers, and suppliers. When Hertz acquired Thrifty and Dollar rental car companies, they were able to exert greater power over their automobile suppliers. Similarly, Proctor and Gamble's acquisition of Gillette gave P&G greater bargaining power with their primary customers . . . WalMart, Walgreens, etc.

- **Expand Geographic Coverage:** Wells Fargo Bank became a national banking institution via a series of acquisitions, including Wachovia which was strong in the southeast United States. Tata Motors (India) secured distribution in the United States and European markets with the acquisition of Land Rover and Jaguar. Entry into foreign markets by acquisition has been particularly vigorous over the past decade.

- **Expand Into New Categories**: Entry into new categories is much quicker via acquisition as opposed to internal development. Pepsi acquired Quaker Oats primarily to enter the large and growing sport drink with the Gatorade brand and product line. The merger of Sprint and Nextel combined consumer and business communications capabilities into a single entity.

- **Quick Technological Access**: Companies lagging the technology curve frequently will acquire companies with needed technology expertise. Cisco, for example, continues to grow by acquiring smaller firms who have developed new technological capabilities, but who lack the capital or expertise to participate in their relevant markets.

How is the acquisition success rate in the United States? Not particularly sterling. It is reported that between 40% and 50% of acquisitions are later divested. A study of over 12,000 U.S. acquisitions revealed that shareholders lost $.12 for every $1.00 invested in an acquisition. Typically, the only shareholders who benefit are those of the acquired company. In most cases, Wall Street recognizes this evidence and the stock price of the acquiring company declines when a pending acquisition is announced.

The following outlines a number of causes for this disappointing track record:

- **Premium or Too High Price Paid:** This is likely the most frequent cause. Newell overpaid for the Rubbermaid acquisition. Pepsi's earnings were diluted by the Quaker Oats acquisition. Daimler acquired Chrysler for $35 billion and several years later sold them to a private equity investor for $7 billion.

- **Related vs. Unrelated Acquisitions:** While I have no empirical evidence to support, I contend that four out of five failed acquisitions are unrelated . . . companies entering markets in which they do not have the experience or expertise to effectively manage. Jim Collins in *Good to Great* talks about staying within the three circles and Tom Peters in *In Search of Excellence* contends firms must "stick to their knitting." Circuit City's purchase of Car Max is a case in point, which is suggested as a major cause of their demise. This makes about as much sense as if WalMart acquired Boeing.

- **Competitive Reaction Negates Benefits:** Too often management does not take into consideration that an acquisition will generate new strategies and actions by the industry competitors, thus reducing or eliminating benefits of the acquisition.

- **Failure to Achieve Expected Asset and Cost Economies:** Management frequently over estimates the favorable impact of consolidation and scale economies. In some instances, expectations are unrealistic, in others, published asset and cost savings is a public relations effort to justify to Wall Street and investors the validity of the acquisition.

- **Loss of Key Personnel:** As soon as a pending merger or acquisition is announced, a flood of resumes begin hitting the streets, both from the acquired and the acquiring company personnel. Employees rightfully become concerned over their future. And, the first to depart are usually the best and most productive employees, as they are most capable of finding alternative employment quickly. To limit key personnel losses, leadership must move quickly after the acquisition or merger to share their strategy with key employees.

71

- **Escalation of Commitment:** Not all acquisitions meet management's expectations. Too often, companies continue to fund and allocate resources to an acquisition that was simply a mistake. Rather than admit the mistake, management will not take the necessary action to divest. For example, Newell acquired Stuart Hall, a consumer and office paper products company. The competitive marketplace would not permit Newell to achieve our minimum profitability standards. Rather than throw good money after bad, we divested the company and accepted the loss on the divested price.

- **Conflicting Company Cultures**: It is not unusual for a company to state that an acquisition or merger has failed because the company cultures were not compatible. To be blunt, that is an **unacceptable excuse for a lack of leadership**! Leadership must establish and communicate their strategy, and if certain people in the organization find the new environment not to their liking, leadership should assist in their departure. As presented by Jim Collins in *Good to Great*, get the right people on the bus and the wrong people off the bus . . . NOW. Do it rigorously, not ruthlessly.

As previously mentioned, Newell's historic success was acquiring struggling companies with a strong market position and turning them around. **Exhibit 10 - 1** outlines the criteria and process employed in selecting and managing acquisition candidates.

Exhibit 10 - 1 The Newell Growth by Acquisition Formula
<ul><li>Basic consumer and office product manufacturing and marketing.</li><li>Common customer universe (i.e. big box retailers).</li><li>Consider both new (stand-alone) and bolt-on businesses.</li><li>#1 or #2 market share in their industry.</li><li>Financially underperforming and/or mismanaged, resulting in a value price.</li><li>Place Newell experienced management team to lead the organization's turn around.</li><li>Install Newell systems and corporate services.</li><li>Ensure organization is lean and flat.</li><li>The newly appointed company president is also the chief marketing officer.</li><li>Customer service is #1.</li><li>Willingness to discontinue unprofitable product categories and customers.</li></ul>Note . . . A bolt-on business is defined as an acquisition that is consolidated with a current business unit.

For more on developing and implementing a strategy for an acquired company, please see **APPENDIX B - Anatomy of a Successful Acquisition**.

Vertical Integration versus Outsourcing

Vertical integration is when firms extend their competitive scope within the same industry. Backward integration is when firms move their operations into sources of supply, such as when Anheuser Busch purchased glass bottle and aluminum can manufacturing companies that were previously suppliers. Forward integration is moving operations toward end users of the final product, such as the numerous outlet malls that continue to expand, featuring retailers like Coach, Nike, Tommy Bahama, etc. Selling direct to consumers via the internet in addition to retailer sellers is a further example.

Outsourcing is the opposite of vertical integration, whereby firms withdraw from certain value chain activities and rely on outside providers to supply needed materials, products, support services, or functional activities. Many companies outsource functions such as information technology, web site construction and maintenance, benefits, maintenance, advertising, and distribution. A "virtual organization" is a company that outsources virtually all activities. For example, Newman's Own is a large not-for-profit company providing food and pet products to the major grocery chains and discount retailers. As of several years ago, they were doing this with less than 20 employees! Essentially everything was outsourced . . . product development, production, marketing, sales, and distribution.

Backward integration may be a viable option if volume is significant, the product or service is critical to the well-being of the firm, suppliers are unreliable or in financial distress, and suppliers are achieving high margins. Forward integration can provide better access to end users, potentially lower distribution costs, or an end user price advantage.

Outsourcing is often the best option when the outside provider can perform the operations better and/or less expensively. American Express outsourced much of their data processing and internet activities to IBM, enhancing performance and saving over $100 million annually! In an acquisition in which I was involved, the acquired company had spent over three years and $3 million in investments (plus engineering manpower) to develop a paint line for their major manufacturing facility. At the time of acquisition, the paint line was sitting on the factory floor and had never been able to paint part number one. The solution . . . we scraped the unusable line and retained an outside company who specialized in the development and implementation of paint lines. The new paint line was up and running in 120 days for a total cost of $625,000. It's not brain surgery!

In addition, outsourcing may be the best option when the activity or function is not crucial to the organization, permitting resources to be focused on areas of expertise and strategic importance. In addition, outsourcing may limit risk exposure, reduce costs, enhance speed to market, and provide access to new products and technologies.

Clearly, the trend is greater utilization of outsourcing and lower levels of vertical integration. As in the case of the paint line example, vertical integration has frequently generated poor results and larger than necessary resource commitments, as organizations frequently do not have the skills or capabilities possessed by outside specialists. Bottom line . . . in most environments, forward or backward integration is not likely to be an attractive strategic alternative.

Offensive and Defensive Strategies

Companies choosing an offensive strategy elect to attack their competition, while a defensive strategy focuses on defending your turf and market position. While an offensive strategy usually receives the most attention, management must be cognizant that **protecting your market position can be just as important a strategy as initiating strategic attacks.**

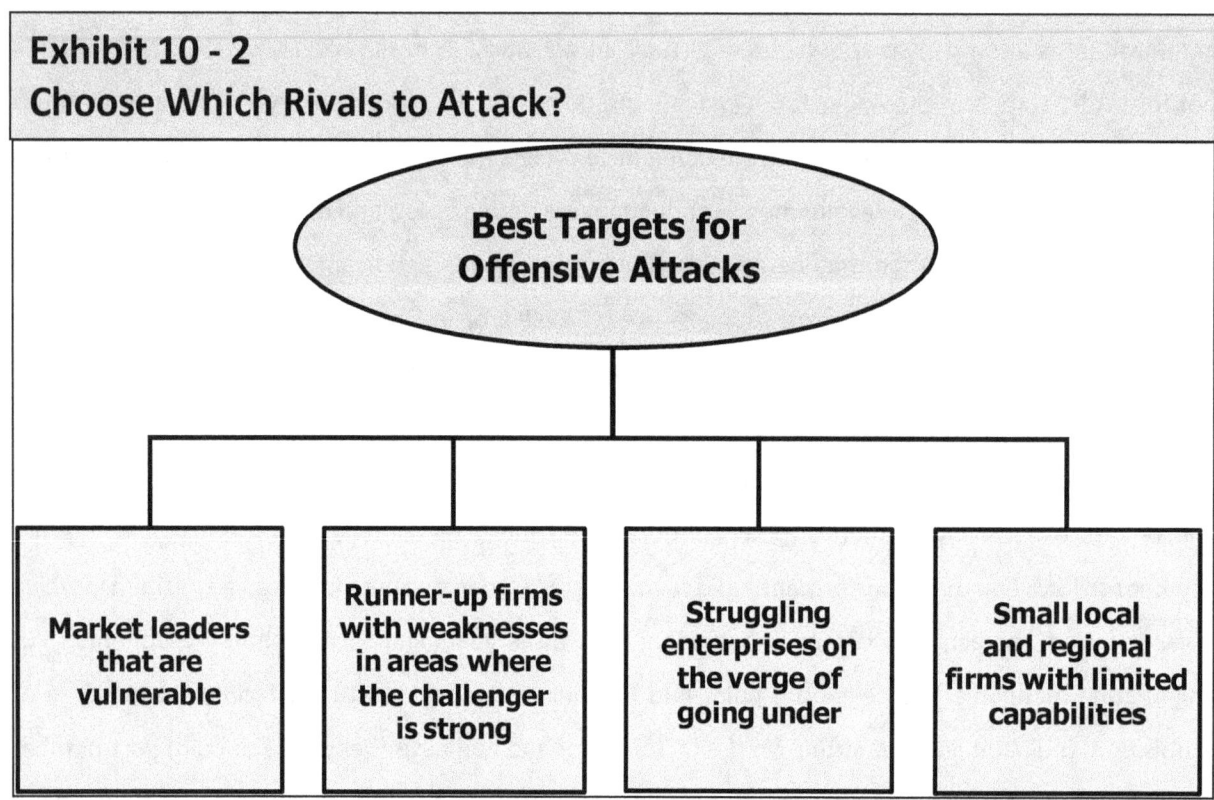

Exhibit 10 - 2
Choose Which Rivals to Attack?

Exhibit 10 - 2 outlines the best targets for offensive attacks. Please note that the common thread is that companies should attack competitive weakness, not competitive strength. Unless there are significant vulnerabilities, management should not mount a competitive attack against the market leader, as their retaliation could be life threatening. Market leader vulnerabilities might include quality issues

74

(Toyota safety issues), poor service, out of stocks, obsolete or dated products, substantial price increases, etc. The timing of an offensive attack can be just as important as the attack itself.

The most common attack strategy is lowering prices. However, unless the firm has a cost advantage, this could result in lower revenue and profits. And, when lowering prices, management must anticipate a competitive response. New and innovative products and/or technologies can also represent a successful offensive strategy. Firms may elect a "hit and run guerrilla warfare" strategy, where management develops a strong and appealing program for one particular customer or market segment. In some cases, like Starbucks, Federal Express, eBay, and Amazon, companies have achieved success with a "blue ocean strategy" . . . creating an entire new industry where market needs are identified and there is no industry or competitor satisfying those needs.

Internet Strategies

There are four basic internet strategies firms can employ, as discussed below.

1. Information Only

An information only strategy precludes selling products or services directly to the end user. Firms will provide education regarding their products and/or services as well as communicating specifications. Many companies will offer direct links for the internet user to contact or purchase from the firm's customers. If your major customers are retailers like WalMart and Home Depot, going into competition with them and selling direct to the end user via the internet is essentially a death wish.

2. Minor Distribution Channel

The internet offers a unique opportunity for market research, to test new product and product concepts, and to evaluate advertising and promotion themes. It can also be an excellent source to market close-out products or products not distributed through the firm's normal distribution channels. As with an information only strategy, this avoids conflict with your existing channel customers.

3. Brick and Click

Bricks are organizations that have physical locations, such as the major retailers and banking institutions. Clicks are using the internet to accept orders and actually sell merchandise or services. Today, virtually all major retailers have a brick and click strategy, selling both from physical store locations and over the internet. While banks continue to have physical locations, the majority of transactions are now conducted via their internet sites. Recent studies have indicated that there is a 10 - 15% cost savings versus the cost of retail locations, which have store personnel, land, building, inventory, distribution, maintenance, etc. costs not fully encountered by internet sellers.

Retailers have had to establish new warehousing and distribution systems to process and ship direct to consumer orders. I consider one of the biggest dropped passes in internet retailing was done by J.C. Penney, who was late to market with their internet web site and store. They had a huge advantage over other big box retailers because they already had the facilities and systems for direct consumer orders through their extensively distributed catalogs. Thus, they could have immediately had a competitive advantage that was missed.

4. **Online Only**

Companies like Amazon, eBay, Priceline, Expedia, Overstock, Net Bank, Monster, etc. have created entire new industries in the past decade. Do not be surprised to find that, within the next few years, over 25% of all U.S. retail sales will be done on the internet. As previously indicated, it is estimated that it is 10--15% less expensive to sell online versus through physical facilities. The one strategic decision internet sellers must address is whether to warehouse and distribute internally or to outsource. Most small sellers elect to outsource or, in the case of some low volume Amazon merchandise, have the manufacturers themselves distribute on their behalf.

Strategies for Different Market Conditions

Depending on the life cycle status of an industry, companies may employ different strategies depending on whether the market is emerging, growing, maturing, or declining.

- **Emerging Industries**

In newly emerging industries, firms have wide latitude in experimenting with different strategies, as little historical information is available. Being first to market and/or out-innovating the competition places firms in an enviable market position. New firms entering the emerging industry have the opportunity to pursue new markets or segments and attract new customers by making it easier or less expensive for end users to purchase and by aggressive advertising and promotion campaigns.

When Apple entered the MP3 market with the iPod (they were not the first to market), they out innovated the competition in both product features and compliments such as iTunes and made the potential market aware of their product offering via creative advertising and merchandising. Apple continues to own an estimated MP3 player market share of 70%, despite maintaining pricing at much higher levels than competition.

Over the past decade, there are a number of examples of emerging industries that have impacted the way we live and work, including electronic banking, e-book publishing, tablet computers, organic foods, online education, long term care insurance, alternative fuels, and a myriad of others.

- **Rapidly Growing Markets**

  In a market that is growing at a fast pace, a firm's strategy must be to grow their revenues faster than the market is growing (i.e. improving market share). This can be accomplished by driving down costs, lowering prices to attract new customer groups, differentiating product, pursuing wider distribution and geographic coverage, and expanding product offerings.

  Vizio did not exist a decade ago. Today they have secured the number one U.S. market share position in flat screen high definition televisions. Major competitive brands were selling 39 to 42 inch models at $2,000 plus and had attracted the early adapter category of purchasers. Vizio drove down costs through their Asian manufacturing sources and offered comparable quality product in the $1,200 range, first through Sam's Club and later to a wide range of major customers (note . . . I still own my original Vizio). The new price point extended the appeal of HD televisions to a broader early majority market, ultimately positioning Vizio as the market share leader.

  Starbucks successful strategy in growing the specialty coffee market is another example. They pursued wider distribution by expanding free standing outlets, placing outlets in airports, retail stores, college campuses, etc., entering international markets, placing product in grocery stores, and expanding their product offering to non-coffee consumables and merchandise.

- **Mature Markets (less than 5% annual growth)**

  In mature markets, the vast majority of buyers are already users and have become more knowledgeable and sophisticated. There is significant head-to-head competition, prices have declined, there is aggressive advertising and promotion campaigns, it is more difficult to maintain profitability, and there are potential mergers and acquisitions among former competitors. Industries like supermarkets, personal computers, and airlines seem to fall into the mature market category.

  A variety of strategic options are available to firms participating in mature markets.

  o Prune marginal products/services. Airlines have discontinued routes with low passenger fill rates. General Motors jettisoned their Oldsmobile, Saturn, and Pontiac brands.
  o Improve value chain activities; improve quality and labor productivity.
  o Implement cost reduction initiatives.

- Increase sales to existing customers. Starbucks continues to expand supplemental products available in their locations in order to increase per customer purchases. Gas stations are now convenience stores, increasing revenue and profits to captive consumers.

- Acquire competitors at a bargain price.

- Expand internationally. Yum Brand's (Pizza Hut, KFC, and Taco Bell) largest market is now China, not the United States. The North American market is saturated with WalMart stores. The only way they could continue to grow was to expand internationally.

- Obsolete yourself. Microsoft introduces new operating systems every several years and replaces existing systems with 'new and better versions'. Golf club manufacturers and many others attempt to obsolete last year's merchandise to induce new purchases.

- **Stagnant and Declining Markets (flat or negative growth)**

Companies participating in mature and stagnant markets are not destined for failure. In fact, in the United States and Western Europe, with slow or no population growth, many, if not most, industries are mature or stagnant. Markets can decline for a variety of reasons such as technological obsolescence (CRT monitors, VHS recording), market shrinkage (baby food), changing lifestyles and tastes (cigarettes, Twinkies, fried foods), or rising costs of complimentary products (large SUVs and cost of fuel). Participants in declining markets have two strategic choices . . . remain committed to the industry or gradually or quickly exit the industry.

For companies in stagnant or declining markets, management can choose one of the three generic strategies. A firm can become the low cost leader by eliminating anything the buyer is unwilling to pay for, aggressively cutting costs, discontinuing marginal products or services, and consolidating facilities and functions. Companies can differentiate in terms of quality, features, styling, etc. P & G (with others following) accomplished this in the toothbrush market by developing and entering the battery operated toothbrush. Instead of consumers purchasing $1.50 toothbrushes, many consumers are now spending $6.00 - $9.00 on the battery-powered version. Again, the most successful companies will combine low cost with differentiation, establishing a best value strategy. In addition, companies can focus their strategy on a strong niche market and vacate the declining broad market. It should be noted, mergers and acquisitions frequently occur in stagnant and declining markets, resulting in consolidation cost savings and greater economies of scale.

If the market no longer represents a viable opportunity, firms may elect to vacate the market. Generally, the best strategy under these circumstances is to harvest cash from the business for as long as possible. Costs and spending are cut to rock bottom levels. Then, when cash flow goes negative or there are additional resource requirements to maintain participation, exit the industry by selling off the company and/or its assets or liquidating.

- **Strategies for Runner-Up Firms**

  A runner-up firm is one whose market share is not in the top three or four in an industry, resulting in weak economies of scale, low customer recognition and preference, limited ability to advertise, and inability to fund expansion. As previously cited, Newell's acquisition strategy was to only acquire companies that had the number one or number two market share in their respective industry (unless they had something unique to offer the market). There is simply too much investment and resources involved to generate greater market share. Keep in mind the adage "only the lead dog enjoys a change of scenery."

  If you are a runner-up firm, attacking the industry leader head-on is seldom a viable strategy. If you are a runner-up and the only way you can compete is on price, your demise is likely to be eminent.

  There are several potential strategies to continue to be a successful secondary participant.

  - **Vacant Niche Strategy . . .** Opportunities exist in niche market where competition is weak or non-existent. However, the niche must be of sufficient size and scope to yield acceptable revenue and profitability. Southwest Airlines was founded on a vacant niche for passenger airline service in Texas. Whole Foods established dominance in organic and natural foods. The niche can also be a market segment, geographic region, or product.

  - **Superior Product Strategy . . .** Examples include Samuel Adams, Chicago Cutlery, Omaha steaks, and Ben and Jerry's.

  - **Distinctive Image Strategy . . .** L.L. Bean, Tiffany, Hummer, Coach.

  - **Private Brand Strategy . . .** There are a number of successful companies who provide the private label (house brand) products to major retailers. Examples include the suppliers of WalMart's 'Best Value' and 'Sam's Choice' products, 'Archer Farms' at Target, and 'Kirkland Signature' at Costco. The range of private label products includes a variety of product categories, including food, OTC drugs, clothing, etc.

- **Strategies for Businesses in Crisis**

  The question for businesses in the crisis mode is whether the business can be saved or is it hopeless. The basis for the crisis can be attributed to mismanagement or a change in the industry environment. Product obsolescence, overestimating sales potential, inability to control both fixed and variable costs, absence of either a price or differentiation advantage, and frequent management and strategy changes are often contributors. In some cases, a powerful competitor can target rivals for extinction. Two decades ago, there were a number of mass merchant chains located in the northeast quadrant of the United States (Ames, Bradlees, Caldor, Hills, Jamesway, and Zayre). Today, all of these retailers reside in the graveyard. They were unable to compete with WalMart and, to a lesser extent Target, who rapidly expanded into their geographic markets.

If the company is unable to develop and execute a strategy to remain solvent in their industry, even after radical surgery to reduce costs, management typically will need to implement a **harvesting strategy** in order to maximize short-term cash flows from operations. Management must cut expenses to the bone, eliminate all capital spending, not replace departed personnel, suspend advertising and promotion, etc. When cash flow goes negative, then the business must be sold if a suitor to purchase the business can be identified or liquidated. Liquidation is certainly an unpleasant option as it represents a hardship on the firm's employees and the communities in which the firm operates.

From an individual business unit standpoint, the recommended format for preparing and finalizing a winning business strategy has been completed. Remember the two most important elements of a successful business strategy:

- **The strategy must improve the company's profitability and financial strength.**
- **The strategy must improve the company's competitive strength and market position.**

Once the strategy is developed, management's job has just begun. They must:

- o Communicate the strategy to stakeholders and employees.
- o Execute the strategy.
- o Establish performance objectives and compensation based on strategy execution.
- o Monitor results and performance.
- o Regularly revise the strategy to changes in the business, industry, and/or market environment.

Subsequent chapters will address international strategies, corporate strategies, and other elements essential to successful strategy execution.

Chapter 11
International Strategies

Why is it important to address international strategies?

> # Answer: 50%
>
> **50% of the revenue of the Fortune 500 U.S. companies is**
>
> **generated outside of the United States!**

Given the importance of participating in foreign markets, this section will provide a brief overview of the complexities of international commerce. Even if your business is managing the corner deli, you will be involved in and impacted by international business transactions.

Exhibit 11 - 1
The World's 30 Most Populated Countries, 2012

World Population: 7,021,836,029

Rank	Country	(000,000)	Rank	Country	(000,000)
1.	China	1,343	16.	Germany	81
2.	India	1,205	17.	Turkey	80
3.	United States	314	18.	Iran	79
4.	Indonesia	249	19.	D.R. Congo	74
5.	Brazil	199	20.	Thailand	67
6.	Pakistan	190	21.	France	66
7.	Nigeria	170	22.	United Kingdom	63
8.	Bangladesh	161	23.	Italy	61
9.	Russia	143	24.	Burma	55
10.	Japan	127	25.	South Korea	49
11.	Mexico	115	26.	South Africa	49
12.	Philippines	104	27.	Spain	47
13.	Vietnam	92	28.	Tanzania	47
14.	Ethiopia	91	29.	Colombia	45
15.	Egypt	84	30.	Ukraine	45

Exhibit 11 - 1 provides an interesting starting point by displaying the world's most highly populated countries. Within the next decade, India is expected to surpass China as the country with the largest population, partially due to China's one child rule. India, in fact, is the world's largest democracy, whereas China remains communist. Russia, by far, represents the world's largest geographic region, while the United States, China, and Brazil are the next largest and are approximately equal size. Interestingly, India's geographic size is only about half the size of the United States, but has nearly four times the population. Until I began teaching International Business, I would have never guessed that Indonesia ranks in the top five countries in population. Indonesia also has the greatest Muslim population in the world.

A frequently used measurement for the standard of living is the country's gross national income per capita. However, to construct apples-to-apples comparisons, this calculation must be adjusted for a country's cost of living and then translated into U.S. dollars. **Purchasing Power Parity (PPP)** adjusts the GNI per capita by comparing the costs of an essential basket of goods (housing, food, medical care, etc.), and then adjusting the calculation. For example, the actual GNI per capita in Norway is over $90,000, but is reduced to $67,000 due to the high cost of the essentials basket. Conversely, due to the lower cost of living in Poland, the GNI per capita is increased to $21,200 from just under $15,000. GNI per capita is shown for select countries in **Exhibit 11 - 2.** Please note that the Democratic Republic of the Congo has the lowest rate of the world's major countries at $400 per capita. Economists suggest that there is a market for U.S. consumer discretionary goods when the GNI per capita exceeds $10,000.

The China GNI per capita, at $9,100, is somewhat misleading, as China is essentially two very different markets. 35% to 40% of their population is centered in major metropolitan areas, where discretionary incomes are much higher than in the rural areas. Lifestyles in this latter region have not changed significantly in the past fifty years (with the exception of mobile phone ownership). Conversely, Russia GNI per capita is also misleading, as the top 10% of the population is very rich, which distorts the overall average for the general population.

To be successful in foreign markets, it is essential that managers understand the culture of the country in which they are intending to have business relations. **Exhibit 11 - 3** indicates the eight major components that comprise the culture of a given country. While a detailed discussion of these components is beyond the scope of this text, it should be noted that religion is the component that is most impactful in determining a country's cultural characteristics. A basic understanding of the major tenets of religious beliefs and practices is vital to success

Exhibit 11 - 2
Gross National Income Per Capita at PPP, 2012; Select Countries

World Average: $12,700		
Norway - $67,000	Japan - $36,300	China - 9,100
Switzerland - $56,200	EU Member Average-$36,000	Indonesia - $4,800
Hong Kong - $53,100	South Korea - $31,000	Iraq - $4,300
United States - $50,600	Russia - $22,700	India - $3,800
Sweden - $44,200	Poland - $21,200	Pakistan - $3,000
Canada - $42,500	Mexico - $16,400	Nigeria - $2,400
Germany - $41,900	Brazil - $11,700	Bangladesh - $2,100
France - $36,700	South Africa - $11,200	D.R. Congo - $400

Exhibit 11 - 3
The Components of Culture

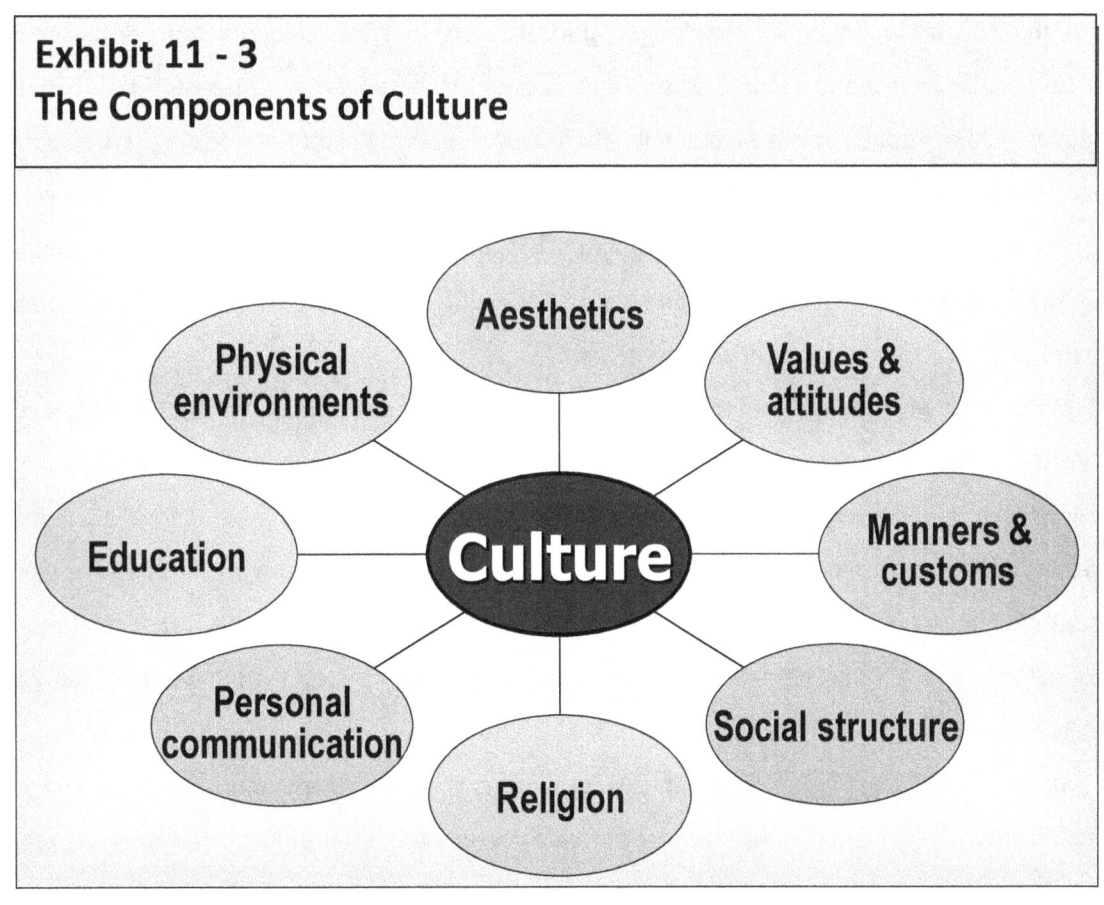

The BRIC + Countries

The four BRIC countries (Brazil, Russia, India, and China), which encompasses over 40% of the world's population, are frequently regarded as representing the greatest opportunity for U.S. products and services. Many have recently added South Africa to this list. My experience in attempting to market in Russia, albeit somewhat limited, suggests this is very difficult and risky market to enter under the current regime and political environment. My preference would be to invest in the central European countries which have or are becoming democratic and have instituted market economics. Poland, Estonia, Hungary, Czech Republic, and others who have been accepted into the European Union would be included. These countries would represent a market of over 120 million consumers who have growing discretionary income.

As displayed in **Exhibit 11-4,** China (frequently termed "The World's Factory") represents an unmatched market for consumer and industrial goods and services. The flat screen HGTV display photo taken at the downtown Shanghai WalMart supports reports that this category represents the single largest revenue source of any product category throughout WalMart China. Also note that the beauty aids section is significantly more fashionable than found in North American WalMart departments. WalMart is regarded as a more upscale shopping experience for the Chinese consumer, further evidence of the growing discretionary income of the population in China's metropolitan areas. On the sourcing side of WalMart, independent reports have indicated that 10% of all exports from China to the United States can be found on WalMart's domestic store shelves.

China is slowly moving from export driven growth to an economy in which Chinese consumers drive growth. For the United States, this represents tremendous opportunities as the 1.3 billion consumers become increasingly able and willing to make discretionary purchases. Those U.S. industries most positioned for growth of the Chinese market include food and agriculture products and equipment, environmental equipment, financial services, health care, education, tourism, and transportation. This growth will result in a rising demand for energy, which is likely to spell higher worldwide prices for imported fuels.

While the India economy will continue to grow, the country's infrastructure remains a decade or more behind China. Port and transportation facilities lag behind the other BRIC countries. However, India is a democracy, with a strong education system being developed as evidenced by the number of "back room" jobs such as call centers, customer service, computer programming, etc. being shifted from the

Exhibit 11 - 4
China . . . The Consumer

Is There Market Potential in China?

- #1 in sales new automobiles
- #1 in sales of new personal computers and tablets
- #1 in sales of new HDTVs
- #1 in sales of new mobile phones and smartphones
- Consumes 33% of world cotton production
- Consumes 51% of world pork
- Consumes 35% of world cigarettes
- Consumes 31% of world coal
- Consumes 50% of world cement
- Consumes 25% of world aluminum
- Consumes 27% of world steel

WalMart - Shanghai

United States and Europe to India. Even MRI's taken in the United States are being read by trained medical personnel in India and accounting firms are having select tax returns being prepared by Indian accountants.

There is strong evidence that the large population and growing economy of Indonesia will present an additional future opportunity for U.S. firms; same for South Africa.

Currency Exchange Rates

Before embarking on a review of strategic alternatives in foreign markets, managers must understand the significant influence exchange rates can have on business operations and decisions.

If the current exchange rate is US$1.35 per one Euro (€), what does that tell us about the strength or weaknesses of the U.S. dollar? The answer is **NOTHING**. $1.35 per Euro is the same as the fact that there are twelve inches in a foot or four quarters in a dollar. The important difference is, while inches and quarters remain constant, currency exchange rates fluctuate over time. Consider the changes between the U.S. dollar and the Euro since Euro implementation in 2002.

2002 . . . €1.00 = $0.90
2006 . . . €1.00 = $1.60
2010 . . . €1.00 = $1.20
2014 . . . €1.00 = $1.35

As an example, if you purchased an item in the Euro zone in 2002 for €10, the equivalent cost in U.S. dollars was $9.00. The same item purchased 2006 for €10 would have cost $16.00! Accordingly, the impact of exchange rate changes has a substantial impact on business decisions.

In discussing currency values, we need to understand the terminology associated with fluctuating exchange rates:

Weak Currency: A country's currency is valued low relative to other currencies.

Strong Currency: A country's currency is valued high relative to other currencies.

Devaluation: Lowering (weakening) of the value of a country's currency.

Revaluation: Raising (strengthening) of the value of a country's currency.

It is imperative firms understand the impact of a devalued or revalued currency as shown in **Exhibit 11 - 5.** If a country's currency is devalued, export prices will decline, making products more competitive in international markets, thus, increasing export volume. However, the price of imports into the country will increase, which will raise consumer prices and limit selection. Conversely, a revalued currency will raise export prices, resulting in higher prices in foreign markets and, thus, reducing exports. Consumers, however, will benefit as prices for imported goods and services decline. **Exhibit 11 - 6** displays examples of this important phenomenon using changes in the value of the U.S. dollar versus the Euro (€)

For financial reporting, firms operating in international markets must convert the financials of all foreign subsidiaries into the home country currency, which can have a substantial effect on reported revenues and profits. Several years ago, Nintendo (Japan) had to adjust their net profits from $2.6 billion to $1.7 billion due to unfavorable currency fluctuations. Consider the dilemma for a company like McDonalds, who must translate over 100 foreign currencies to U.S. dollars every month.

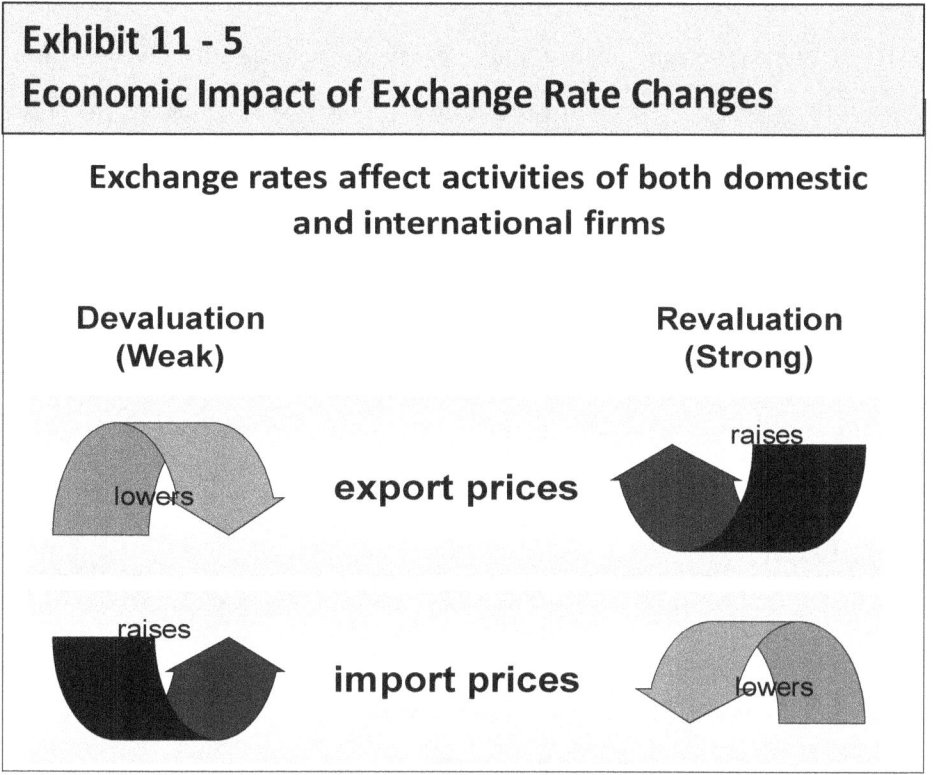

Exhibit 11 - 5
Economic Impact of Exchange Rate Changes

Exchange rates affect activities of both domestic and international firms

Devaluation (Weak)		Revaluation (Strong)
lowers	**export prices**	raises
raises	**import prices**	lowers

Exhibit 11 - 6	
Impact of Currency Devaluation and Revaluation . . . Examples	
U.S. Dollar Devaluation	**U.S. Dollar Revaluation**
What happens if the U.S.$ weakens from $1.25 per € to $1.50 per €?	What happens if the U.S.$ strengthens from $1.25 per € to $1.10 per €?
• U.S. exports will be more appealing and exports will increase. A product selling for $10.00 now costs €6.67 rather than €8.00.	• U.S. exports will be less appealing and exports will decrease. A product selling for $10.00 now costs €9.09 rather than €8.00.
• U.S. import prices will increase and consumer buying power and selection will decline. A product selling for €20.00 will now cost $30.00 rather than $25.00.	• U.S. import prices will decrease and consumer buying power and selection will increase. A product selling for €20.00 will now cost $22.00 rather than $25.00.

Weak or devalued foreign subsidiary currency reduces earnings when restated to the home currency. For example, what happens if the euro devalues from 0.75 per U.S. dollar to 0.85? If revenue from the European subsidiary was €1.0 million, revenue translated to U.S.$ would be $1.18 million (1mm/.85) versus $1.33 million (1mm/.75).

Strong or revalued foreign subsidiary currency, on the other hand, improves revenues and profits when restated to the home currency. For example, what happens if the euro revalues from .75 per U.S.$ to .65 per U.S.$? If revenue from the European subsidiary was €1.0, revenue translated to U.S.$ would be $1.54 million (1mm/.65) versus $1.33 million (1mm/.75).

In addition, in comparing year-to-year revenues and profits, companies must utilize a common exchange rate to ensure apples-to-apples comparisons. Certainly stable and/or predictable currencies make financial planning, forecasting, and cash flows much easier to manage, while reducing unfavorable currency exposure risk, like the Nintendo example. Currency speculators constantly exchange currencies, attempting to profit from exchange rate fluctuations. I suggest you would have better success at a Vegas craps table.

The China Dilemma

For many years, exporters, manufacturers, and governmental officials in both the United States and Western Europe have been pressing the government of China to allow the Chinese RMB (¥ or commonly called Yuan) to float freely in international markets. Historically, the Yuan was pegged to the U.S.$, trading in a narrow range averaging ¥8.0 per $1.00. Over the past decade, the Chinese government, under pressure from the United States, has allowed the Yuan to strengthen to a recent level of ¥6.15 per $1.00. The result has been an escalating cost of Chinese goods and services, igniting firms to reconsider either making product domestically or searching for other lower cost international alternatives.

Consider the following example. The company has been manufacturing and purchasing product from a Chinese company at a cost of ¥100. When the exchange rate was 8¥ to the dollar, the cost of the product was $12.50. Today, the cost of the same ¥100 product is $16.26 at ¥6.15 per U.S. dollar. In addition, the full cost of the product has increased further, as there have been significant increases in freight costs due to raising petroleum costs and the supply and demand for ocean freight containers. Import tariffs are usually levied as a percent of product costs, fueling further cost increases.

The bottom line is that U.S. made products and services are more competitive both at home and abroad. In theory, this should favorably impact the tremendous trade deficit with China, but China must ease their restrictive import policies for U.S. products and services. The United States continues to purchase approximately $4.00 of Chinese imports versus our $1.00 of exports to China.

Why Companies Expand Internationally

Exhibit 11 - 7 outlines why companies elect to enter international markets. Gaining access to new customers is doubtless the most common reason. When domestic markets become saturated, the most obvious vehicle to sustain growth is to enter international markets. For example, the United States and

Canadian markets are virtually saturated with WalMart stores. In Flagler County, Florida, where I reside, we have one WalMart Supercenter. If another store is opened, WalMart sales in Flagler County will not double, as sales from the new store will bastardize the existing store sales, yielding only an estimated

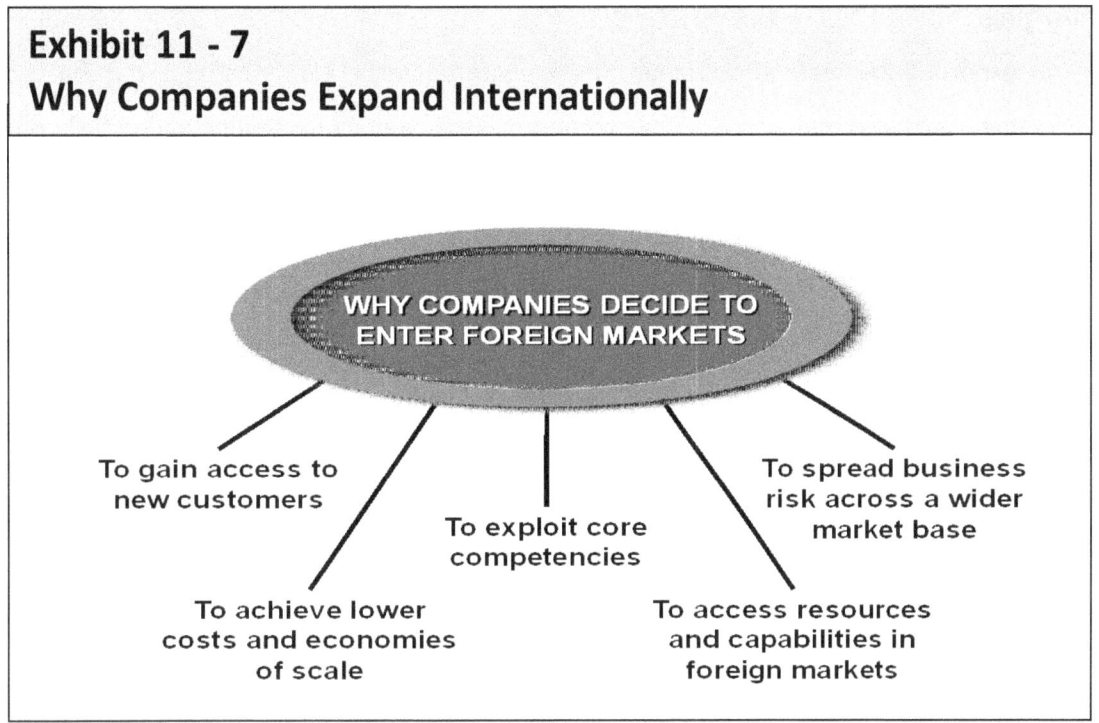

Exhibit 11 - 7
Why Companies Expand Internationally

WHY COMPANIES DECIDE TO ENTER FOREIGN MARKETS

To gain access to new customers

To exploit core competencies

To spread business risk across a wider market base

To achieve lower costs and economies of scale

To access resources and capabilities in foreign markets

30-35% sales increase. For that increase, the high cost of constructing a new store outweighs the aggregate sales increase. Accordingly, the only way for WalMart to sustain growth (and keep Wall Street happy) is to enter new markets where true incremental sales potential is available.

Companies can be categorized as an international competitor where there are operations in a select few companies (WalMart) or a global competitor where there are operations in 50 or more countries with plans to expand further (McDonalds).

Foreign Market Entry Strategies

There are several different methodologies for entering a foreign market, as outlined below. No matter which entry methodology is used, companies that enter emerging foreign markets, with low discretionary incomes, the preferred strategy is typically to compete on the basis of low price. If the demographics dictate limited market potential, companies should avoid entering such markets.

We are now seeing greater incidence of global brands, using the same brand worldwide. For example, InBev is in the process of establishing Budweiser and Stella Artois as global brands. Marlboro is the number one cigarette brand worldwide, even though the actual product is adapted for local tastes. Companies just now embarking on global expansion usually begin their quest close to home. For U.S.

firms, typically Canada is the starting point, followed by Mexico. For example, Walmart began their international expansion in Canada, followed by Mexico, the United Kingdom (same language and similar shopping preferences as the United States), and then to Germany and Asia.

- **Exporting**

  An exporting market entry strategy means using domestic plants as a production base for exportation to foreign markets. This can be an excellent strategy for testing and initially pursuing international sales. It is a conservative alternative that minimizes risk and initial capital investment, as well as not requiring direct investments in foreign countries. External marketing agencies who are knowledgeable and have local country contacts are often employed, as the company itself lacks the necessary expertise.

  Exporting strategies can be vulnerable, however, as manufacturing costs in the home country may be higher than in foreign countries where rivals have facilities. High shipping costs, restrictive government policies, and financial or other requirements can further reduce success opportunities. As discussed previously, adverse fluctuations in currency exchange is a potential threat.

- **Alliances and Joint Ventures**

  Alliances and/or joint ventures with a foreign country partner helps avoid startup costs and potential barriers to entry. This approach allows for resource and risk sharing, while learning the particulars of operating on foreign ground. The partner's knowledge and contacts in local markets can be invaluable, if the right partner is selected. The alliances or joint venture can be either contractual or verbal, with verbal agreements and understanding, in many Asian countries, being more important than written contracts.

  The cost and time to establish a working agreement can be restrictive, particularly in Asian environments where negotiations can last for extended periods, which tend to frustrate Americans who are more impatient than their Asian counterparts. Protection of proprietary technology or patented processes can also be a concern. Disagreements when there is joint control can be troublesome. Cultural and language barriers can also limit understanding and agreement. While minor details can be handled via the telephone or computer technology, there is no substitute for frequent face-to-face contact with the alliance partner.

- **Licensing and Franchising**

  In many software and pharmaceutical markets, companies will license the right to manufacture and/or market in foreign locales. This can be a valid strategy when the company does not have the capabilities to enter the market themselves or to avoid high entry costs and potential risks. The downside of licensing is that control over business and technology can be lost and a competitor can actually be created.

Franchising has largely been a phenomenon created by U.S. companies, but it is beginning to become a more frequent strategy in Europe. Franchising tends to work best in service and retailing environments, where the majority of costs and resources are born by the franchisee. The franchisor usually assumes responsibility for recruiting, training, and monitoring the franchisee. In some cases, depending on local preferences and tastes, the franchisee may need the freedom to modify the marketing mix. The ability to maintain quality control is a constant concern of franchisors.

The international franchisor with whom most of us are familiar is McDonald's, who now operates franchises in roughly 150 countries. Other major franchisors included YUM Brands (KFC, Taco Bell, and Pizza Hut), Starbucks, 7-Eleven (huge convenience store throughout Asia), and many hotel chains. McDonald's and Pizza Hut, for example, do allow menu modifications for local tastes. Beef burgers do not sell well in Hindu countries (replaced by mutton) and U.S. consumers would probably not be motivated by having sea slug as a pizza topping, which is popular in Taiwan.

Franchisors and licensors generally charge either royalties or a fixed percent of revenue in order to generate income. For example, YUM brands reportedly charges franchisees a 5% royalty on revenue plus another 5% of revenue for advertising and marketing support.

- **Acquisitions and Greenfield Investments**

International acquisitions occur when the domestic company purchases and manages the operations of a foreign firm. A greenfield investment, on the other hand, involves entering a foreign market by building the business from the ground up. For example, since there was no applicable acquisition candidate, General Motors made a greenfield investment and built a factory and operations in Poland in order to enter the Central European automobile market.

The number one advantage of an acquisition is speed to market, as operations, organization, distribution, customers, technologies, etc. are already in place. As long as government agencies approve, which can be cumbersome, the normal array of entry barriers and their associated costs and complexities can be avoided. The major acquisition challenge, however, is integrating the acquired firm's structure, cultures, policies and procedures, and personnel. From personal experience, foreign company management and employees often resent being managed by "foreigners." I have seen, on too many occasions, American business people entering a foreign country and conveying that they are from the United States, we're smart, and we're going to tell you how to conduct business. This is a certain recipe for failure. Observing and learning before action is required to be successful. And, if the culture of the company is at odds with the country's culture, the country culture will win.

A greenfield investment is the slowest form of entry due to the extended period of time to secure various governmental approvals, construct facilities, develop and train an organization, and establish distribution channels and a customer base. If new facilities are required, capital costs can be restrictive. Depending on the country's political and social environment, instability and a lack of legal protections can disrupt operations.

International Marketing Strategies

In entering international commerce, companies must understand consumer tastes, preferences, buying habits and purchase criteria can be very different, even among bordering countries. Market size and growth potential, as well as distribution channels, can vary significantly, as well. One of the biggest concerns for companies competing in foreign markets is whether to customize their product offerings in different markets to match the tastes and preferences of local buyers or offer a mostly standardized product worldwide.

The goal of virtually all companies participating in international markets is to standardize as much of their product or service and marketing strategy as possible in order to achieve the lowest possible cost basis. While full standardization is possible for items such as watches, perfume, and luggage, some modification is frequently required to meet local needs. Consider the following examples:

- Electrical Products . . . the vast majority of the world is 220 versus 110 voltage in the United States, plus, plug configurations are different in different regions.

- Automobiles . . . While auto configuration can be very different from region to region, Toyota has been successful in minimizing costs and inventory requirements by having 60% of internal parts being standardized worldwide.

- Refrigerators . . . Whirlpool, like Toyota, has standardized as many internal components as possible despite external configurations being different. In southern Europe, for example, refrigerators are very small, as most households purchase fresh goods on a daily basis. In China, refrigerators have decorative styling and bright colors, as they are a status symbol frequently located in the household's living room.

- Mobile Phones . . . In Islamic markets, smartphones must be loaded with the Koran, an alarm to signal prayer time, and a compass in order to point toward Mecca.

- In Asian countries, the number one flavor of ice cream is green tea. (It's not bad!)

Some strategies and products are not suitable in select markets. Ownership of clothes dryers is low in Italy, as households typically prefer to hang clothes to dry. WalMart failed in Germany, as German consumers viewed shopping there was an admission that they were in a low social - economic class, plus greeters were viewed with skepticism. Preferences can be different within a country or region, as well. Costco, with others recently following, offer two versions of Coca-Cola in their southern U.S. markets; the traditional formula and a formula that is sweeter and utilized pure sugar cane, which is preferred by the Hispanic market.

Accordingly, companies have three general strategic alternatives when entering foreign markets:

1. **Think Local, Act Local**

    Vary the product offering and competitive approach from country to country, where tastes and preferences are different. Under this alternative, it is difficult to achieve low cost leadership due to limited economies of scale. Local managers, therefore, have considerable latitude in strategy development and decision making.

2. **Think Global, Act Global**

    Under this alternative, the same product, brands, and marketing strategy are offered worldwide. This strategy yields the greatest opportunity for economies of scale and low cost leadership.

3. **Think Global, Act Local**

    This common strategy requires modifications for different countries or geographic regions who have unique requirements, but where the firm standardizes as many components as possible. This is the approach used by Toyota and Whirlpool in the examples cited above. VW, for example, utilizes the same expensive-to-produce video in their TV advertising in all markets, but simply changes the inexpensive voice over to the local market language.

Foreign Sourcing and Manufacturing

From an outsourcing standpoint, where products or services are purchased in foreign markets and sold in the domestic market, the driving force is lower product and service costs. The vast majority of the Fortune 500 manufacturing companies have strategic alliances, joint ventures, wholly owned subsidiaries, or all of the above in China. Many companies have jumped on the bandwagon and blindly began sourcing products and/or services in the Pacific Basin. For U.S. companies, sourcing in Mexico or Central America may actually be less expensive, even if per unit costs are higher. Savings in transportation, inventory requirements, travel, etc. can outweigh a lower base cost. Similarly, European countries should investigate alternative sources in Central and Eastern Europe for the same reasons. And, for high labor content products, firms should also evaluate automation in their domestic operations. As previously noted, we are beginning to see a rebirth of 'Made in America' products due to escalating freight costs and strengthening of foreign currencies.

Companies must consider that different countries can have very different location appeals. Wage rates, worker productivity, inflation rates, energy costs, tax rates, and government regulations must be researched. **Exhibit 11 - 8** displays the average total hourly wage cost, including benefits, in select countries. Labor costs in China are expected to begin significantly increasing, which is driving China factories to lower labor cost areas such as Vietnam and the Philippines.

Exhibit 11 - 8
Average Hourly Total Labor Costs for Select Countries; 2011

Vietnam	$0.30	Hungary	$5.00
China	$0.80	United States	$23.82
Russia	$2.00	Canada	$25.74
Mexico (higher at border)	$2.75	Germany	$34.21
Brazil	$4.91	Norway	$41.05

Concentrating Versus Dispersing Global Activities

To gain the best competitive position, should the company concentrate activities in a few locations or disperse them to many locations? **Exhibit 11 - 9** outlines the market circumstances that will define the best alternative. In some cases, there are particular countries that have special capabilities, such as production of computer motherboards in Taiwan, decorative wood products in Malaysia, leather products in Brazil and Italy, perfume in France, and brass plated products in India.

Exhibit 11 - 9
Concentrate or Disperse International Activities?

Concentrate Activities When:	Disperse Activities When:
<ul><li>Lower costs</li><li>Products highly standardized</li><li>Significant economies of scale</li><li>High capital investment</li><li>Steep learning curves</li><li>Limited resource availability</li><li>Low distribution costs</li><li>Few trade restrictions</li></ul>	<ul><li>Products/services are multi national</li><li>Limited scale economies</li><li>Low capital investment</li><li>Resources readily available</li><li>High distribution costs</li><li>Volatile exchange rates</li><li>Unstable political environment</li><li>High trade barriers</li></ul>

Johnson and Johnson manufactures their contact lenses in a single U.S. facility. The factory is highly automated, there are rigorous quality standards, the product is the same worldwide, distribution costs are negligible, and there are limited foreign government trade restrictions.

Conversely, Whirlpool appliances are manufactured in 72 plants and 17 countries throughout the world. It's expensive to ship refrigerators, washers, and dryers thousands of miles across oceans. The plastic residential playground equipment made by Little Tykes is manufactured in the United States, even though it can be made in China for about one-half of the U.S. cost. Cost to ship these large items that have low value density make China total costs higher.

Government Trade Policies

Governments establish both restrictive foreign trade policies as well as incentives to promote foreign trade. Such policies can have a significant impact on potential trade relations, which must be understood by management and factored into the decision process.

- **Restrictive Government Trade Policies**
  - **Import Tariffs and Quotas**

    The driving force in establishing import restrictions is to protect domestic producers from foreign competition. In some cases, particularly for poor countries, it is a means of generating money for the government. The most common restrictive policy is import tariffs or quotas. An import tariff requires that the foreign producer pay the government of the importing country a percent of the value of the goods entering their market. For example, if Taiwan levies a 10% tariff on foreign produced automobiles, the auto manufacturer must pay the Taiwan government 10% of the cost of the vehicle. If the vehicle's cost is $30,000, the manufacturer must pay $3,000 upon arrival at the port in Taiwan. The tariff can either be a percent of unit cost or in the case of bulk product, so much per unit of weight.

    A quota is a limitation on the amount of a good that can enter a country. For example, for many years, the United States had a quota, or maximum limit, on the amount of textile products that was allowed to enter the country from China. In some cases, government's levy a quota tariff. For example, the tariff on the first million units entering a country is 3%, for the second million units the tariff is 6%, and in excess of two million units, the tariff is 8%.

  - **Export Tariffs and Quotas**

    While not as frequent as import restrictions, export tariffs and quotas are implemented by governments usually to ensure domestic demand and needs are met when local resources are in short supply. These restrictions are frequently levied on local agricultural products in order to guarantee the domestic population can be fed.

  - **Local Content Requirements**

    Governments establish local content requirements, usually specifying a percent of the value of the product must come from local sources. Frequently, this requirement is for the labor content of the product in order to preserve or generate domestic jobs.

o **Regulation on Pricing of Imports**

Governments and/or the World Trade Organization (WTO) will regulate pricing on imports if there is evidence of dumping or unfair government subsidies. Dumping is defined as attempting to sell products to select foreign markets at or below cost or lower than prevailing prices in other markets. For example, several years ago the European Union (EU) found that Chinese and Vietnamese manufacturers were marketing shoes in the EU at below prevailing prices. The EU, in response, placed a two year tariff of 14% on Chinese and 11% on Vietnamese shoes entering EU countries. Some countries will place what is termed 'countervailing tariffs' on foreign products believed to be receiving unfair government subsidies. Because it places local producers at a disadvantage, it is not uncommon for countries to place such tariffs on subsidized U.S. agricultural products.

o **Other Restrictive Regulations**

In some instances governments will establish technical or composition standards on certain products, where domestic manufacturers meet the standard, while potential import products do not. At Newell, the German government, at the request of domestic manufacturers, established plastic composition standards for food storage products that German manufacturers met, but import product did not. For many years, Coca Cola did not participate in the soft drink market in India as the government required the specific formulation of Coke, which is the company's most carefully regarded secret. Governments can also implement complicated and time consuming certification standards before a company can import into the domestic market. In other instances, slow or delayed customs clearance requirements can make exporting impractical. U.S. organizations have sent produce to needy African nations, only to have the produce rot in warehouses awaiting customs clearance.

- **Government Trade Incentives**

Conversely, governments often offer incentives to encourage trade and investments. A foreign government, frequently local, will offer some or all of the following investment incentives:

o Tax waivers or reduction

o Low or no cost land

o Construction subsidies

o Infrastructure improvements

o Worker training

o   Technical assistance

o   Access to local markets

Why does a government offer these types of incentives? Simple . . . the incentives are given in exchange for local jobs, which further enhances the local economy. Ireland is reported to have the world's best pro-business environment for investment, with low taxes, incentives, and a responsive government. Why does Mick Jagger live in Ireland? Taxes are a fraction of those in England.

Many U.S. states offer these types of incentives to entice both foreign and domestic investors. Tennessee has historically been the most aggressive state in inducing potential investment. Several years ago, we pitted Illinois versus Michigan to determine which state would offer the greatest incentives for us to retain an existing facility and relocate a new distribution center. Illinois was selected because they offered the most lucrative package of incentives, which resulted in a very unpleasant conversation with the governor of Michigan.

Regional Economic Integration

Regional economic integration has and continues to change the landscape of the global marketplace. It is the process whereby countries in a geographic region cooperate either to reduce or eliminate barriers to the free flow of products and services, which has resulted in the opening of new markets and the availability of goods and services not previously available or too expensive to be meaningful. As shown in Exhibit 11 - 10, there are five levels of economic integration ranging from the most integrated (political union) to the least integrated (free trade area).

Exhibit 11 - 10
Levels of Economic Integration

Political Union	Coordinate aspects of members' economic and political systems
Economic Union	Remove barriers to trade, labor, and capital; set a common trade policy against nonmembers; and coordinate members' economic policies
Common Market	Remove all barriers to trade, labor, and capital among members; and set a common trade policy against nonmembers
Customs Union	Remove all barriers to trade among members, and set a common trade policy against nonmembers
Free-Trade Area	Remove all barriers to trade among members, but each country has own policies for nonmembers

- **Benefits and Potential Drawbacks of Economic Integration**

    When trade barriers are reduced or eliminated, the level of trade increases among members, resulting in a wider selection of goods and services available at a lower cost, which results in higher demand. In addition, because the integrated countries are economically married, it is easier to achieve greater consensus and the potential for political or military conflict is substantially reduced. Proponents of regional integration believe jobs are created and wages are raised, increasing the standard of living and quality of life, particularly in developing countries.

    The most controversial aspect of trade integration is the potential shift in employment, as jobs move to those countries with the lowest labor rates. In the case of the North American Free Trade Agreement (NAFTA), the U.S. government claimed that the integration with Mexico created approximately one million jobs in the United States. Trade unions, on the other hand, claimed that one million jobs were lost. The reality is that it was probably close to a zero sum game. However, in this instance, most agree that higher paying U.S. manufacturing jobs were lost to Mexico, but were replaced with lower paying employment in the service sector, which also required retraining of skill sets. In both NAFTA and the European Union (EU), it is clear the least skilled jobs were relocated to the lowest wage locals.

    Another potential result is trade diversion, where trade between integrated members increase, while trade with countries not included in the agreement is reduced. For example, even when the U.S. dollar was weak, reducing the real cost of U.S. goods and services, trade declined with EU member countries as trade within the EU increased in the absence of trade barriers. Those opposing trade integration are also concerned with the loss of individual country sovereignty and independence.

    Whether one agrees or disagrees with the expansion of regional economic integration, it is and will continue to be a fact of the global business environment, and managers must learn to understand and operate within the new complexities of this environment.

- **The European Union (EU)**

    The foundation of the EU was established in 1951 with the Treaty of Paris, where a handful of Western European countries banded to reduce trade barriers in order to assist in rebuilding Europe following World War II. Various forms of integration followed, culminating with the establishment of the EU as an economic union and implementation of the euro (€) currency beginning January 1, 2002. Members have removed barriers to trade, labor, and capital, have set common policies against non-members, and now coordinate economic policies.

98

As of January 1, 2014, there were 27 Western and Central European nations who are EU members, with several additional countries applying for membership. Future members must meet certain criteria, including being a democracy, having a market economy, and having stable institutions of human rights and laws, with strong economic and monetary policies and positions. There are four Western Europe countries who have elected not to join the EU, most notably Norway and Switzerland, plus Iceland and Liechtenstein. While not members, these countries do abide by the majority of EU criteria and rules. Of the 27 countries, 17 have established the euro as their official currency. The remaining ten have either elected not to transition to the euro (UK, Sweden) or have yet to meet the required economic criteria. The 27 participating EU countries represent a market of 500 million people.

Implementation of the euro has eliminated exchange rate risk among participants, and has certainly reduced the cost and complexity of currency conversion. At the Newell companies for which I was responsible in Europe, prior to the establishment of the euro, we had to convert 16 currencies to U.S. dollars every month in order to close our books, versus only seven currencies after euro implementation.

Since people with the EU may choose to live and work in any country they desire, this has created issues in high labor rate countries such as German, France, and the UK, where immigrants from Central Europe have moved westward and are displacing local workers. In addition, many European consumers believed, in the transition from their local currency to the euro, companies seized this as an opportunity to disguise price increases.

- **North American Free Trade Agreement (NAFTA)**

    Beginning in 1994 and fully implemented in 2008, the United States, Canada, and Mexico, under NAFTA, agreed to remove all trade barriers, while each country maintained their own policies with non-members. Encompassing 450 million people, the agreement included complex rules of origin, local content requirements, government procurement practices, granting of government subsidies, intellectual property rights, and standards of health, safety, and the environment. Unlike the EU, there is no free flow of labor between members.

    As previously noted, the results of the agreement have generated a great deal of controversy, particularly regarding worker displacement. Since full implementation, there has been a 300% increase in U.S. imports from Mexico and a 200% increase in U.S. exports to Mexico, yielding a significant U.S. balance of trade deficit. While U.S. trade with Canada has grown, trade relations were already at a very high level, suggesting that NAFTA had nominal impact. Many manufacturing jobs have moved south since implementation, including companies with whom I was involved. While Mexico's health, safety and environmental standards have improved, they fall short of established United States and Canadian domestic standards. One should keep in mind, there can be a large difference between legislating standards and actual implementation and enforcement.

What is the future of NAFTA? Both the Clinton and Bush administrations promised that they would approve the addition of Chile, which is a model for economic and social progress in Central and South America. The political winds, however, have stalled this expansion for fear of unfavorable public reaction and purported loss of jobs, which in reality is essentially nonsense. Chile is geographically distant from the U.S., has only 14 million people, and 90% of our trade with Chile is already free. The impact would be insignificant, but the message extremely important to other South and Central American countries.

In my opinion, if we do not aggressively pursue additional membership, the major South American countries will continue to grow their trade agreements among themselves or with Europe, thus excluding the United States from these lucrative and growing markets, who have rapidly expanding middle classes. To make such expansion impactful, Brazil, with 200 million people that represents 60% of South America's population, must be included. Brazil, however, still needs certain economic and market reforms. The next two largest nations, Argentina and Columbia, would need to follow. We should recognize Brazil's official language is Portuguese, not Spanish, as in all other Central and South American nations. I regarded this as an important alternative for students considering learning a second or third language.

There has been some reference to the potential establishment of the FTAA . . . the Free Trade Agreement of the Americas, which would include 800 million people from the northern tip of Alaska to Tierra del Fuego in South America. The United States has been the primary pitcher of cold water on these discussions, with politicians fearing protests from environmentalists, labor and worker's rights organizations, etc. I am certainly fearful if we continue building a trade fence around our country, the long term viability of our economy will be seriously jeopardized.

Chapter 12
Corporate Diversification Strategies

To this point, the majority of this guide has addressed developing business strategies for single business units. This chapter will present developing a corporate strategy for firms with multiple business units. A corporate strategy is simply the umbrella over which a diversified corporation manages various business units. Why do firms diversify? To create added value for stakeholders by building a multi-business company whose whole is greater than the sum of the parts and to reduce risk from having all their eggs in a single basket. **The bottom line . . . to make 1 + 1 = 3.**

The following are the most common forces driving a business to diversify.

- o **Slow growth in the current business** . . . to sustain growth, WalMart had to expand business operations to international markets, as they reached near saturation in North America.

- o **Enter new product categories** . . . Apple has gone from a computer company to a multi-dimensional powerhouse through entry into the MP3, music download, mobile communication, and tablet markets.

- o **Enter new technologies** . . . this has been Cisco's growth driver.

- o **Leverage existing competencies and/or capabilities** . . . Bright House Networks was a supplier of cable TV service and, since they already had lines running to customer homes, expansion into DSL service, phone land lines, and home security was natural diversification.

- o **Powerful brand transfer to other businesses** . . . Honda expanded their purview into other motorized vehicles, including motorcycles, ATVs, and mowers and small tractors.

There are three basic methodologies that firms can employ to enter new businesses:

1. Acquisitions

The most common diversification comes via acquisitions and is often the best choice if the price is justifiable. It is usually the fastest approach in entering a new business or market, as facilities, personnel, distribution, brand name, etc. are already in place. However, it is not uncommon for companies to pay 30-40% over the firm's market cap for the business, which can actually dilute earnings. Attractive acquisition candidates include companies with undervalued assets, companies in financial distress (particularly those with a strong market position), and companies with bright growth prospects but lack necessary investment capital.

2. Internal (Greenfield Investment)

Companies can also diversify either through the establishment of new company or internal development of new product categories that establishes a new business venture. This approach can be highly time consuming and expensive, as capital investments, facilities, personnel, distribution, etc. must be built from ground zero. Obviously, if the diversification represents an innovation or creation of a new industry, this form is required. Otherwise, management must ensure that a strong market position can be acquired, either through a low cost position or significant differentiation, particularly where there is vulnerable or weak competition.

3. Joint Venture

When a company, for whatever reason, is unable to diversify alone, a joint venture can be established with another firm who has the necessary knowledge and capabilities to proceed. Within the United States, the venture is often based on the acquisition of special technology from the venture partner. It is also frequently found for both sourcing from foreign markets (usually to secure the lowest possible cost) or to enter foreign markets.

As shown in **Exhibit 12–1**, there are **two primary types of diversification ...related and unrelated.**

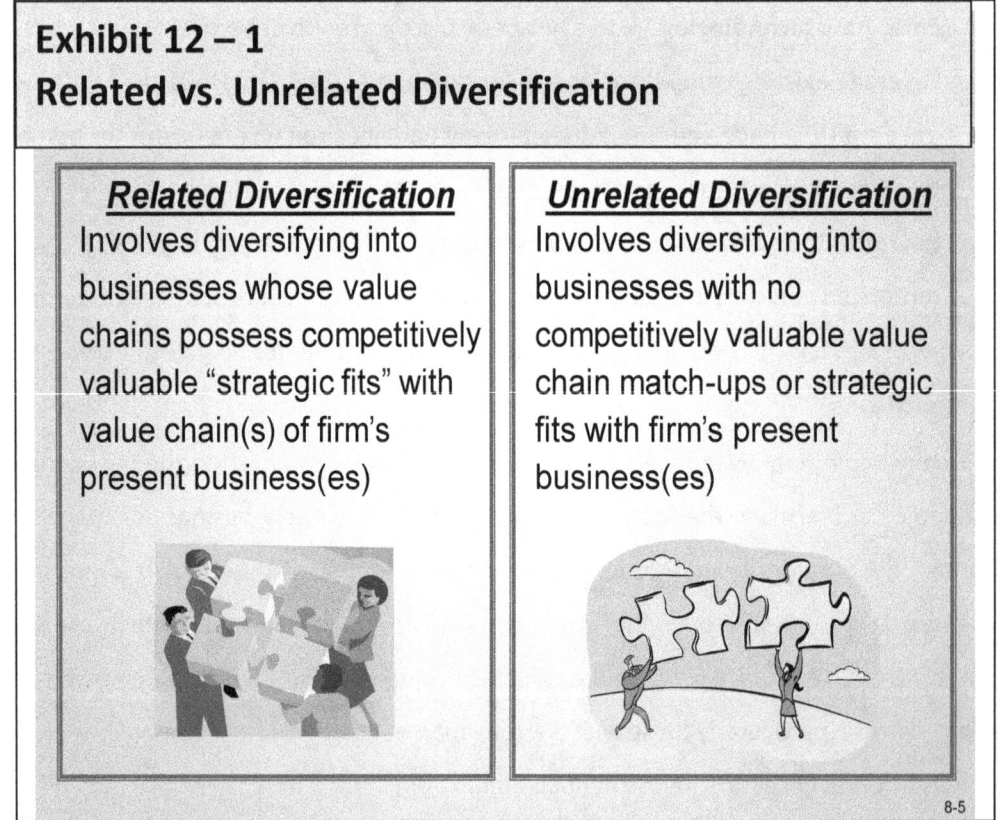

Exhibit 12 – 1
Related vs. Unrelated Diversification

Related Diversification
Involves diversifying into businesses whose value chains possess competitively valuable "strategic fits" with value chain(s) of firm's present business(es)

Unrelated Diversification
Involves diversifying into businesses with no competitively valuable value chain match-ups or strategic fits with firm's present business(es)

8-5

Related Diversification

The basis for related diversification is to make 1 +1 = 3 by transferring capabilities from one business to another, sharing facilities and resources, leveraging the use of a common brand name, consolidating business activities and functions, and spreading risks over a broader business base. As displayed in **Exhibit 12 – 2**, the strategic fit in the firm's major functions reduces operating costs and leverages revenue growth.

Exhibit 12 – 2
Value Chain Strategic Fit

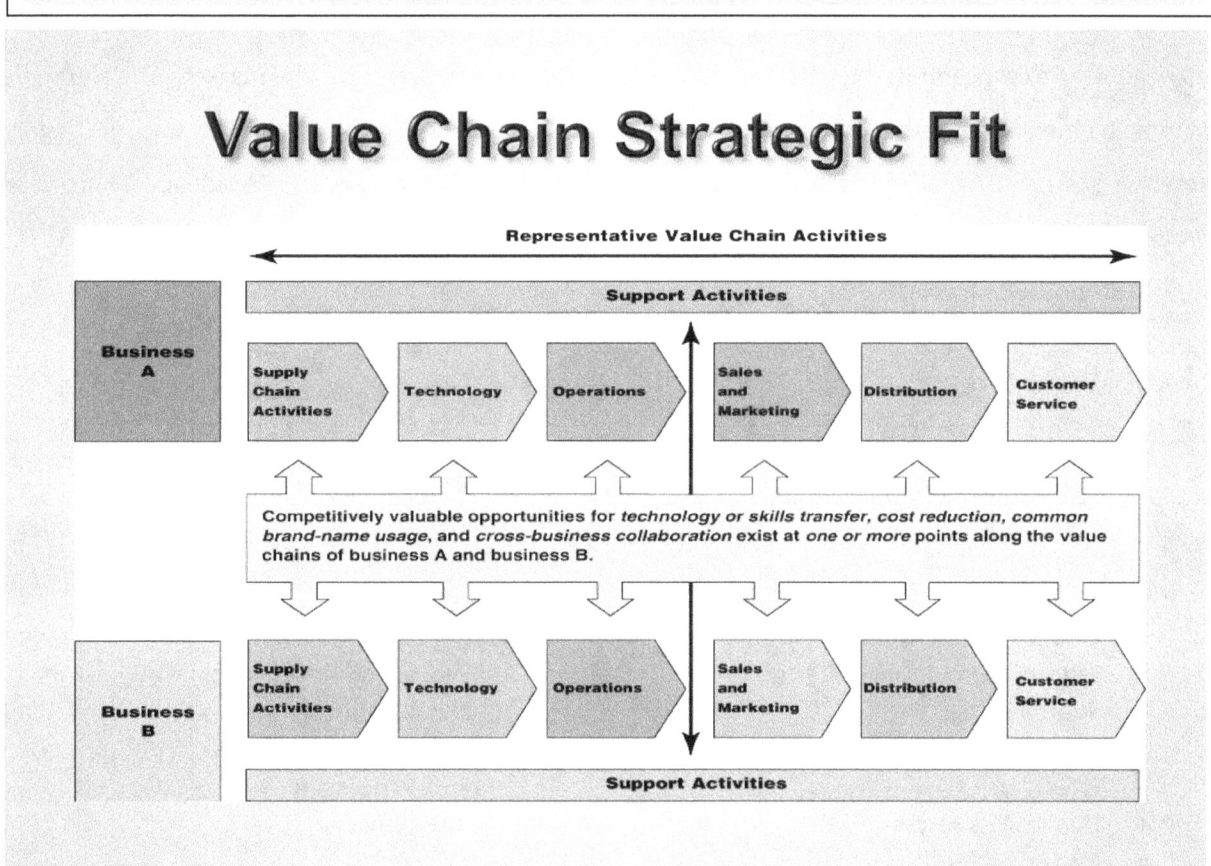

Newell's diversification strategy represents an excellent example of related diversification, via growth by acquisition. The framework for their strategy was to acquire companies that:

- Manufactured or sourced and marketed everyday products for the home and office.
- Products sold predominately to the big box retailers (i.e. WalMart, Home Depot, Penney, Staples, etc.}

- Held the #1 or #2 market share in their industry (or had developed new and unique products).

- Could be acquired for a depressed cost due to underperformance and/or weak management. The company strived to make both stand-alone acquisitions that would allow entrance into new markets and would be a separate operating entity, and bolt-on acquisitions, where the acquired firm would be consolidated into an existing business unit.

As shown in **Exhibit 12 – 3**, each individual Newell business unit was a free-standing company with its own organization, supported by secondary corporate service functions for which each business unit was levied a 2% of revenue charge. With over 20 divisions selling to the same general universe of customers, there was no need to have 20 different credit, tax, legal, investor relations, etc. functions at the business unit level. The cost savings to the corporation was substantial, while freeing business unit management to concentrate their activities on what was really important . . . the market. The hierarchy of management above the business unit level totaled eight people, so each unit was run highly autonomously. Business units were divided into three groups headed by a Group President . . . Hardware Products, Household Products, and Office Products. After a number of acquisitions, a fourth group, Newell Europe, was formed.

Exhibit 12 – 3
Newell's Organization Strategy

Business Unit Activities	Corporate Service Activities
• Management • Sales • Marketing • Finance and Accounting • Manufacturing • Sourcing • Distribution • R & D • Human Resources • Customer Service	• Tax • Credit • Legal • Benefits • Payables and Receivables • IT and Accounting Systems • Investor Relations • Payroll Processing • Acquisitions

Unrelated Diversification

Unrelated diversifying involves entering businesses with no strategic fit, no meaningful value chain relationships or unifying strategic theme. The basic approach is to diversify into any industry where the potential exists to realize favorable financial results. Accordingly, unrelated diversification is a finance driven strategic approach, while related diversification is a market driven strategy. The primary criteria for unrelated diversification via acquisition should be targeting companies that:

- Meet corporate profitability and return objectives, or can be restructured to achieve financials.

- Participate in growing industries.

- Are large enough to significantly contribute to the parent company.

- Have manageable capital requirements.

- Are free of union and labor issues.

- Are not highly vulnerable to economic and other variables.

Acquisition Facts and Opinions

The facts regarding acquisitions in the U.S. are quite clear . . . 50% of acquisitions fail! The only winners in the acquisition sweepstakes are the stakeholders of the acquired firm. The stakeholders of the acquiring firm lose an average of 12% of every dollar invested in an acquisition. The most common cause of failure is overestimating the potential, both market and financial, and under estimating (or not projecting) competitive reaction.

While there is no empirical evidence to verify, it is the author's opinion that four out of every five failed acquisitions is an unrelated acquisition. Why? Management does not understand the business and marketplace or know how to manage in an unfamiliar environment. Unlike related diversification, there are no cross-business value chain or market opportunity advantages or synergies. In some cases, such an acquisition results in management energies being directed to the acquired firm, while focus is lost on the base businesses. This was certainly the case with Circuit City, where management efforts were deflected to the acquisition or Car Max, while Rome was burning at the hands of Best Buy and subsequently Amazon.

Often management claims the cause of the acquisition failure was "incompatibility of cultures." Sorry, but this is simply an excuse for poor and indecisive leadership. Management must immediately establish and communicate their vision and mission for the business and define who and how the business will be managed. Those in the acquired organization must then either commit to the new direction or depart for greener pastures. Often, management is afraid of alienating personnel, which results in unclear direction and competing functional areas. In the words of Colin Powell, "By procrastinating on the difficult choices, trying not to get anyone mad, and by treating everyone 'nicely', you'll simply ensure the only people you'll wind up pissing off are the most creative and productive people in the organization."

Diversification Strategy Analysis

In evaluating a firm's diversification strategy, management must address the following questions:

- Is the industry attractive?
- What are the competitive strengths of each business unit?

- Are there cross business strategic fits?

- Do we have the financial resources required to fund the business?

- How do the business units rank from best to worst?

- What strategic moves are required to enhance overall corporate performance?

The following exercises can assist management in answering these critical questions.

- **Industry Attractiveness Analysis**

    In **Exhibit 12 – 4**, a sample industry attractiveness matrix is shown. On the left axis are those factors most important to the organization in evaluating the strength of an industry. Each factor is then weighted relative to its importance, where the intensity of the competition usually has the strongest weight (typically 20-30%). Factors and weights can be different from company to company. Then, each industry is ranked from one to ten on each factor, with one being very unattractive to ten being highly attractive industry. A weighted total score is then calculated for each industry. This analysis can be constructed for both participating industries as well as prospective industries. Scores less than 5.0 suggest the industry is not particularly attractive.

Exhibit 12 – 4
Industry Attractiveness Analysis

Factors	Weight	Ind. A	Ind. B	Ind. C	Ind. D
Size + Projected Growth	10%	8	5	2	3
Intensity of Competition	25%	8	7	3	2
Opportunities + Threats	10%	2	9	4	5
Cross Industry Strategic Fit	20%	8	4	8	2
Resource Requirements	10%	9	7	5	5
Seasonal/Cyclical Issues	5%	9	8	10	5
Economic + Social + Regulatory Factors	5%	10	7	7	3
Industry Profitability	10%	5	10	3	3
Risk + Uncertainty	5%	5	7	10	1
Weighted Industry Attractiveness Score	1 – Unattractive 10 – Very Attractive	7.20	6.75	5.10	2.95

In the above matrix, Industries A and B are quite attractive, while Industry C is in the middle of the attractiveness scale. Industry D does not appear to be an industry that management would wish to enter.

Exhibit 12 – 5
Business Unit Strength Analysis

Factors	Weight	Co. A in Ind. A	Co. B in Ind. B	Co. C in Ind. C	Co. D in Ind. D
Market Share	15%	10	1	6	2
Cost Competitiveness	20%	7	2	5	3
Product Attributes	5%	9	4	8	4
Strategic Fit with Sister Businesses	20%	8	4	4	2
Leverage Over Suppliers	5%	9	3	6	2
Brand Image + Reputation	10%	9	2	7	5
Value Chain Capabilities	15%	7	2	5	3
Profitability vs. Competition	10%	5	1	4	4
Weighted Competitive Strength Score	1=Very Weak 10=Very Strong	7.85	2.30	5.25	3.15

- **Business Unit Strength Analysis**

    Step two of the analysis is to prepare a business unit strength matrix. As shown in **Exhibit 12 - 5**, on the vertical axis, list those factors most important for a company to be successful against their competition. Then assign an importance weight to each factor. Rate the firm's business units on each factor, with ten being very strong and one being very weak. Finally, calculate a weighted total score for each company. A score of 6.7 or higher indicates the company has a strong market position, like Company A. A business unit with a score of score of 3.3 – 6.7 has moderate competitive strength (Company C), while a score of 3.3 or less, describes a company with weak market positions (Companies B and D).

- **Combined Analysis**

  The final step in the diversification strategy analysis is to combine the two prior matrices into a nine cell industry attractiveness and competitive strength matrix, as shown in **Exhibit 12 – 6**. Industry attractiveness scores are plotted on the vertical axis, while the business unit strength scores are plotted on the horizontal axis. The size of the plotted ovals are proportional to the percent of total company revenue generated by each business unit.

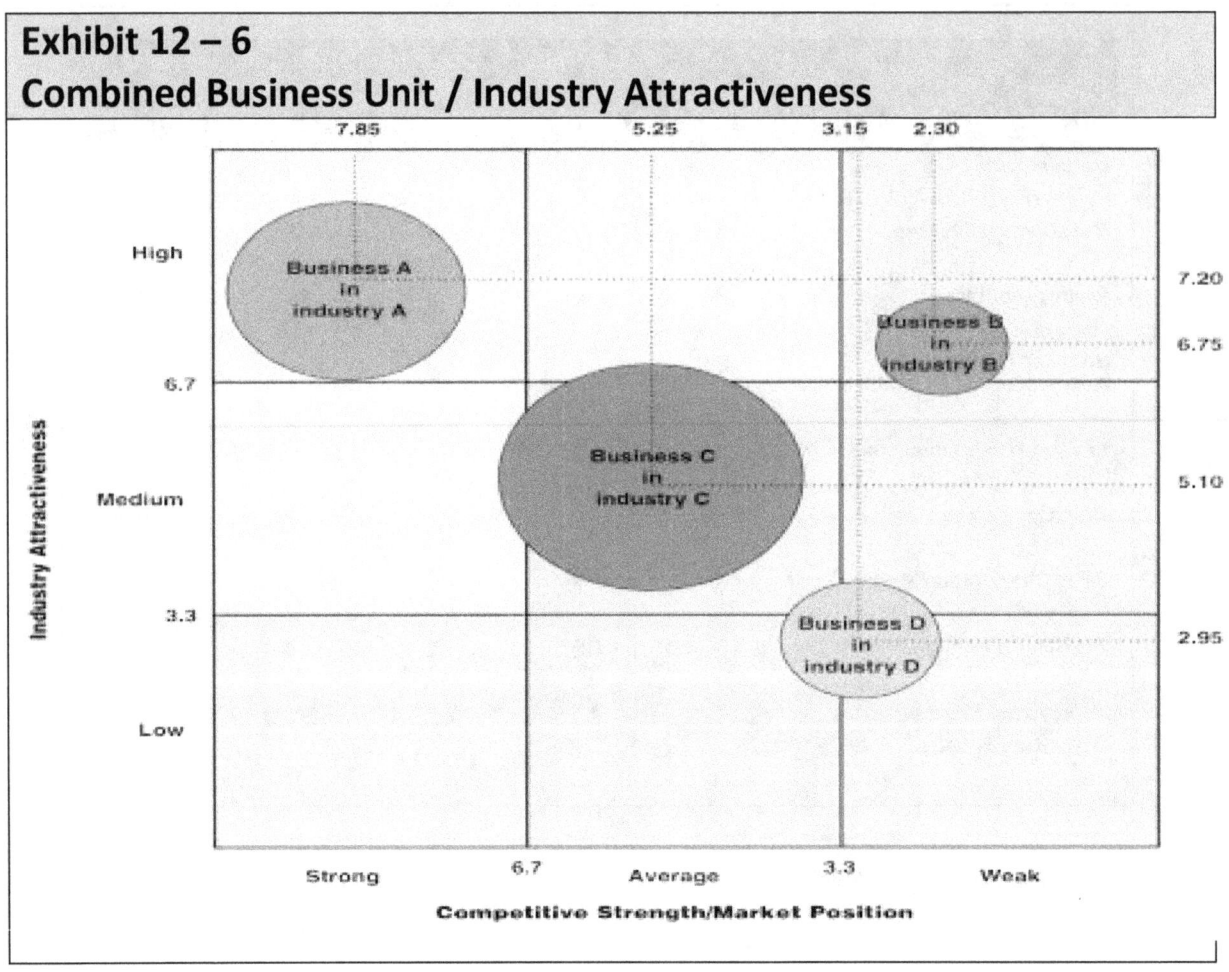

Exhibit 12 – 6
Combined Business Unit / Industry Attractiveness

Company A . . . 7.20 Industry and 7.85 Company Strength:

> This is the firm's second largest business unit, with a strong position in a strong industry. This is likely the corporation's "star" business unit, where the strategy should be to grow and build. Company A should, therefore, be first in line for resource allocation.

Company B . . . 6.75 industry and 2.30 Company Strength

> Company B is a weak player in a fairly strong industry and is the firm's smallest business unit. Because of the attractiveness of the industry, management needs to assess if this

company can become a "Star." If so, significant resource allocation may be warranted in order to grow the business. If not, only moderate resource allocation is appropriate.

Company C . . . 5.10 Industry and 5.25 Company Strength

This is the firm's largest business unit with moderate strength in a moderately attractive industry. Caution is warranted here, as this is likely to be the firm's "Cash Cow" (more later) and sufficient resources should be allocated to ensure continued productivity. The cash generated from the business can be used to fund business growth in other areas.

Company D . . . 2.95 Industry and 3.15 Company Strength

This is a relatively small business unit having a weak position in an unattractive industry, and is likely to be the firm's "Cash Hog." Unless this unit is very profitable and requires limited resource support, Company D should be allocated minimal resources. Management should consider potential divestiture of this business.

BOTTOM LINE . . . Allocate resources where you can maximize long-term stakeholder wealth.

Strategic Fit

Management should also consider the strategic fit of existing or potential businesses. The matrix shown in **Exhibit 12 – 7** attempts to evaluate where strategic fits among business units has the potential to create revenue generation and cost savings opportunities.

Table 12 – 7 Cross Business Strategic Fits						
	Sales and Marketing	Distribution	Operations	Purchasing	Technology	Service
Business A						
Business B						
Business C						
Business D						
Business E						

- There are potential sales, marketing, and distribution synergies between companies B, C, and D. Sales force consolidation? Brand sharing? Shared warehousing and shipping? Umbrella advertising? Common merchandising? Common customer service?

- In operations, can companies A and D consolidate manufacturing? Engineering? Quality assurance? R&D?

- Can companies B and D combine purchasing efforts to secure lower prices? Better deliveries? JIT inventories?

- Can companies A and B share technology and related skills?

- Should companies B and D establish consolidated call centers? Return departments? Repair centers?

- There are no strategic fits between company E and the four other business units. Management must assess if this fits the firm's overall business strategy and profitability requirements. If not, consideration may be given to divestiture.

Cows and Hogs

Cash Cow business units generate cash surpluses over what is needed to sustain their present market position and financial contribution. Such businesses are valuable because the surplus cash generated can be employed to pay corporate dividends, finance new acquisitions and market entries, and invest in promising cash hog businesses. Management must keep cash cows healthy and fortify and defend their market and financial position.

Cash Hogs, on the other hand, generate internal cash flows that are inadequate to fully fund working capital and new capital investment requirements. Accordingly, the parent company has to continually pump capital into the business unit to "feed the hog." Management essentially has two strategic options in addressing cash hogs. Aggressively invest in attractive cash hogs with significant market and financial potential or divest cash hogs who lack long-term potential.

Common Failures

Not every diversification action or acquisition is successful. Several of the most common causes of failure include:

- **Escalation of Commitment**

    Escalation of commitment is the failure to admit the company has made a bad acquisition or new market entry or have cash hogs with limited future potential AND continuing to commit resources. Often managerial egos result in throwing good money after bad rather than face the reality that the diversification move was not successful. Were all of Newell's acquisitions successful? Of course not. However, once realized the acquisition could not meet financial standards or was not a strategic fit, management acted swiftly to divest the acquired company.

- **Overestimating Strategic Fit Savings**

    Often corporations are too aggressive in projecting both the timing and the savings from strategic fit opportunities. In some cases, management reports optimistic future results in order to justify to stakeholders and the investment community the value of the diversification. It is not a perfect world and management must establish conservative expectations. Management stated that there would be a one billion dollar consolidation savings resulting from the merger of Delta and Northwest Airlines. Time will tell if this was a realistic projection.

- **Underestimating Competitive Reaction**

    One of the primary reasons for overly optimistic projections is not recognizing that competition will respond to the company's acquisition and diversification actions. Management should ask the question "How would we respond if our primary competitor did this?"

Crafting New Strategic Actions

In developing a new or updated strategy for diversified corporations, management may decide to take one of the following strategic approaches:

- Stick closely with the existing business lineup and pursue opportunities as they become identified.
- Broaden the company's business scope by aggressively making new acquisitions in new industries.
- Divest (sell, spin-off, or liquidate) certain businesses and retrench to a narrower base of business operations.
- Restructure the company's business lineup, with major changes in the business unit portfolio.
- Pursue multinational diversification in order to globalize operations of select business units.

Whichever future strategy is selected by the diversified corporation management must ensure:

Diversification MUST enhance shareholder and stakeholder value

AND

1 + 1 must equal 3

Chapter 13
Organization and Culture

"A second-rate strategy perfectly executed will beat a first-rate strategy poorly executed every time."

To be successful, companies must ensure they have the organization in place capable to both support and execute the strategy, particularly when major strategic changes need to be implemented. And, the job of executing the strategy is the job of the entire management team, not just a few senior executives. Crafting the strategy is primarily a market-driven activity, while executing the strategy is predominately an action oriented operational activity. Radical changes to the strategy requires a very different execution and organization commitment than for minor changes or adjustments to the strategy. Just because senior management announces a new strategic direction does not mean organization members will embrace it and move enthusiastically forward to implement it. **Exhibit 13 – 1** outlines what management must do to successfully implement a new strategy.

Exhibit 13 – 1
Executing the Strategy

What Executives Have to Do . . .
Unite the Organization Behind the Strategy

- *Communicate* the case for change
- Build *consensus* on how to proceed
- Arouse company-wide *enthusiasm* for the strategy crusade
- *Empower* subordinates
- Establish progress *measurements*
- *Reward* achievements
- *Direct resources* to the right places
- Personally *lead* the strategic change process

The quality of the organization's people is an essential ingredient of successful strategy execution. According to Jim Collins in *'Good to Great'* (see Chapter 14), *"People are not the organization's biggest asset . . . the right people are. Get the right people on the bus, get the wrong people off the bus, and get the right people in the right seats. Only then can you drive the bus in the right direction."*

Staffing the Organization

For a strategy to be successfully executed, firms will frequently need to recruit outside the existing organization. Please keep in mind, if the organization currently has qualified and talented personnel, the first choice should always be to promote from within. You already know the strengths and weaknesses of current organization members, which you can never fully assess for external candidates. Promoting from within has the added benefit of sending the right message to the organization regarding internal advancement potential.

In evaluating external talent which is more important . . . experience or accomplishments? Experience or intelligence? Experience or motivation? It is my opinion, as is the opinion of many successful companies like Google, Amazon, Microsoft, Nike, GE, P&G and others, accomplishments, intelligence, and motivation are much more important than experience. If a candidate has ten years of experience, is that really ten years or is it one year of experience ten times? While somewhat controversial, I am a strong believer in testing managerial and professional candidates as part of the hiring process. We would employ an industrial psychologist to both interview and assess candidate intelligence and personality by administration of standardized tests. If you have an organization staffed with people of average intelligence and drive, you will strive for mediocre results. Hire only the best and brightest, capable of both developing sound strategies and then getting in the trenches to implement the strategy.

Consider ranking organization member on an 'A – B – C – D' basis. 'A' players are the horses you want to ride in order to achieve outstanding results. Give them challenging assignments, promote them, and compensate them well. 'B' players are those you should strive and mentor to become tomorrow's 'A' players. The average, or 'C' personnel, should be challenged and driven to become 'B' players within the next six months. If they cannot become 'B' contributors, replacement should be a strong consideration. For 'D' players, a 30 to 60 days probation period is warranted. If immediate improvements cannot be made, they should exit the organization. Note there was no mention of 'F' ranked personnel. If the organization has such personnel, they must be removed from the organization NOW. And, exit consideration should be given to the managers of 'F' players for allowing severe underperformance. Keep in mind, everyone in the organization knows who the weak performers are. If you, as a manger, tolerate substandard personnel, you will lose the respect and confidence of your superiors, peers, and subordinates and risk jeopardizing your career.

Training has become an integral part of improving the talent of organization members, as well as an important element in retaining key employees. Orientation programs, internal universities, tuition reimbursement, professional development courses, and professional certifications have become standard fare in many high performing companies. General Electric is acknowledged as having the world's best training and development program through their Management Leadership Center.

Cooperation between organization functional areas is also critical, as there are few mutually exclusive activities. Consider something as simple as filling a customer order. Sales, customer service, finance, supplier inputs, production, warehousing, and distribution must work together to ensure customers are satisfied with their purchase experience. However, manageable conflict is an essential element in high performance organizations. An organization free of conflict becomes stagnant and apathetic in the absence of leadership that allows disagreement and the willingness to embrace change.

Trends in Organization Structure

A firm's organization structure is the arrangement of tasks, responsibilities, and reporting relationships. While organizations have formal organization structures and charts, the informal structure is often just as critical to success as the formal structure.

In a **centralized organization** structure, top executives make all of the strategic and important decisions. In a **decentralized organization**, decision authority is pushed down the organization to the lowest capable level. The trend is and continues to be toward greater decentralization because:

- Authority rests in the hands of those who have the greatest local business unit knowledge and expertise.
- Fewer organizational layers, placing key managers closer to customers and end users.
- Higher levels of employee motivation and satisfaction.
- Encourages greater employee initiative and involvement.
- Greater organization creativity and innovation.

In most environments, there is significant evidence that high levels of centralization is a recipe for failure. High levels of centralization, formalization, and bureaucracy often compensate for a lack of talent in the organization. In large, multi-dimensional corporations, complete decentralization is virtually impossible. While certain activities and procedures need to be prescribed, important decisions regarding those issues that impact individual customers and marketplaces need to remain local, where the greatest knowledge resides.

Span of control, the number of subordinates a manager can efficiently and effectively direct, goes hand and hand with the trend toward greater decentralization. The trend is to wider spans of control,

114

where managers are assigned a greater number of subordinates, thereby reducing the number of managers and related personnel costs. Consider the example shown in **Exhibit 13 - 2**, where each company has a total of 4,096 operatives at the lowest organization level. The first company has an average span of control of four, resulting in six management levels and 1,365 managers. The second company, with an average span of eight, has only four managerial levels and 585 managers, or 780 fewer managers. If the average cost of salary and benefits for managers is $60,000, the second company is spending $46.8 million less on management personnel.

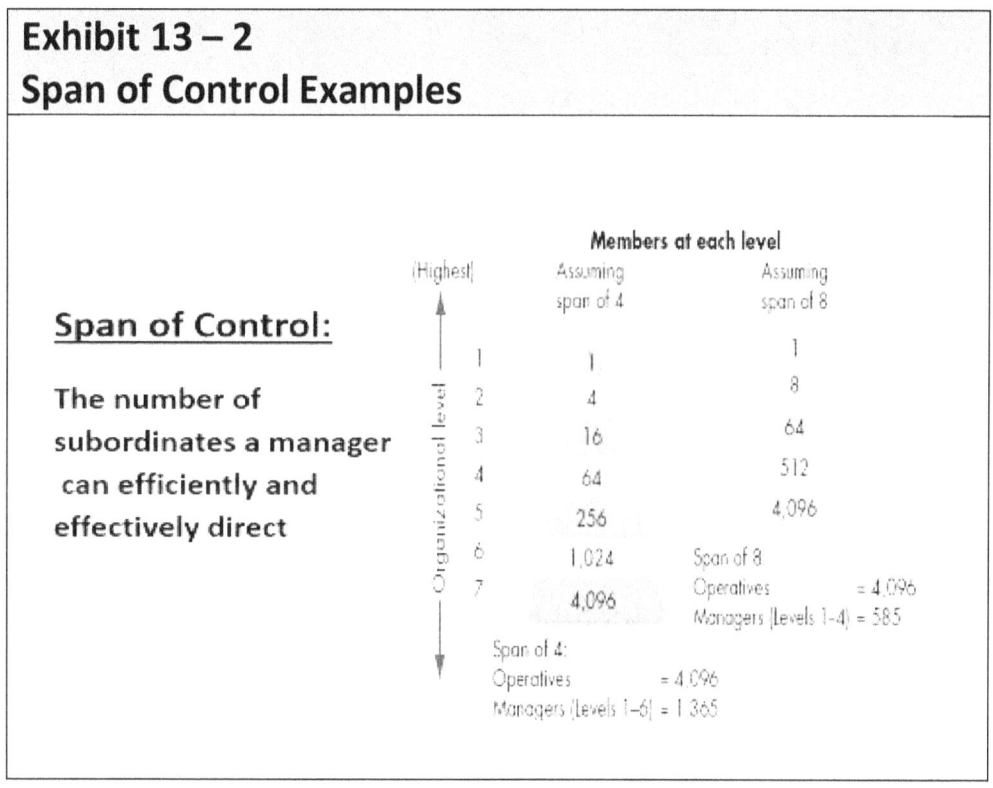

In addition to the financial savings of wider spans, communications are slower and more complex, top management is further removed from the marketplace and customers, and employee motivation tends to be lower due to overly tight supervision. However, the company must ensure employees get adequate leadership and support. It should be recognized there are no "ideal" spans of control, as effective spans can be different depending on the company, the types of jobs, and the nature and competence of the workforce.

Other organization trends include greater outsourcing rather than vertical integration, telecommuting, and job sharing.

Monetary Rewards and Incentives

Today, over 70% of companies offer incentive bonuses for both managerial and non-managerial employees (vs. only 20% in 1980). Incentives must relate to performance and results, not just showing up for work and doing one's assigned job tasks. For example, if a university is paying their football coach a salary of $2 million, I would prefer to pay the coach a base of $1 million and an incentive bonus of $100,000 per win, thus compensating for the results achieved.

The following are guidelines in designing incentive compensation programs:

- Benchmark base compensation versus the local market and like industries to ensure the company is competitive.

- Incentive programs must extend beyond just the top executives. "I want you to work your ass off next year so that my spouse can have a new Mercedes" just doesn't cut it!

- The incentive opportunity must be objective, fair, and achievable . . . but must also be a stretch beyond normal expectations.

- The incentive program must be linked to the company strategy and its related financial and market objectives.

- Participants must be able to impact the outcome. If your business unit represents 10% of overall company sales, basing the incentive program on total company performance is ineffective, as you have little impact on the outcome.

- The realistic incentive opportunity should represent a significant portion of total compensation. 10% to 12% should be the minimum. If 5% or less, there is little or no motivational impact. 20% plus will really get employee attention.

- Walk the talk. Installing a $90,000 hand-made Persian rug in the CEO's office the same day a salary freeze is announced is not a good idea (true story). No more limos or traveling secretaries, please. If you are operating in a union environment, no more German executive cars (this was not one of my most popular decisions).

- No exception, no excuses. If your largest customer went out of business, then go find a new one. If you make exceptions and adjust an incentive plan for one or a few individuals, where do you draw the line?

Non-Monetary Benefits

While monetary rewards are important, providing attractive benefits can be just, and sometimes more, crucial in retaining and motivating employees. First and foremost is flexible health care benefits at a reasonable cost. Flexible coverage means employees should be offered a matrix of alternative coverage based on household characteristics and differing levels of coverage. Second, retirement savings programs, such as 401k programs or other voluntary contribution plans, is a critical element, particularly with the virtual elimination of fixed pension programs and the dubious future of Social Security. Third, training programs to advance employee knowledge and capabilities and remaining technologically current is becoming a frequently mentioned benefit important to employee satisfaction. Additional benefit elements, such as tuition reimbursement, telecommuting, flexible scheduling, job sharing, and compressed workweeks, have become valuable benefits, particularly to two working household heads facing work-life and child-raising conflicts.

While tangible benefits are important, so are intangible benefits. Making liberal use of non-monetary rewards such as formal and informal praise and recognition can be a major contributor to employee satisfaction and retention.

Company Culture

A company's culture is the character of the organization's internal values, work climate, personality, and traditions. The culture can either be an ally or an obstacle to strategy execution and is particularly challenging with mergers and acquisitions. **Exhibit 13 – 3** outlines the characteristics of strong and weak company cultures.

Exhibit 13 – 3
Strong versus Weak Cultures

STRONG CULTURE:	WEAK CULTURE:
• Emerge over period of years	• Lack of shared values
• Clear business philosophy	• Few behavioral norms or traditions
• Values widely shared by all employees	• Frequent leadership changes
• Behavioral peer pressure	• Little cohesion among functional areas

• Genuine concern for:
   • Employees
   • Customers
   • Shareholders
	• Lack of employee allegiance

• Management "walks the talk"	• Hinders strategy execution
• Reinforced by rewards and recognition	• Easier to change than a strong culture
• Employee "fit" crucial	

A strong culture is often established by a strong founder or leader and related stories, as is the case with Sam Walton at WalMart. The morning WalMart cheer, pursuit of low costs, frugal operating practices, a strong work ethic, mandatory Saturday headquarters meetings, and one day per week in stores for buyers are all part of the Sam heritage.

In weak cultures, the company is just a place to work in order to make a living. Companies with weak cultures tend to be resistant to change, have highly political and bureaucratic environments, are focused internally rather than on the end user, have self-interested leadership and low ethical standards. I experienced a memorable example of a weak culture on a visit to Kmart's former headquarters in Troy, Michigan. A major competitor had significantly reduced prices in attempt to secure a portion of our 100 plus SKUs at WalMart. Knowing the competitor would make the same attempt at Kmart, we went to Kmart with a price reduction that would add well over $1 million in incremental profit for them. The buyer's response was "God dammit, Thomas, why are you doing this to me. Do you realize it will take me two full days of work to enter and implement the change? Don't ever do this to me again." And you wonder why WalMart has and continues to erode Kmart's business.

Changing a company's culture can be a challenging undertaking. It is particularly difficult to change a culture that is strong, while a weak culture is actually easier to change and establish a new one that will be welcomed by employees. Cultural change in international environments can also be tricky, as U.S. management may not be well versed in both the business and country culture in a particular locale. And, if there is a conflict between the company's culture and the country's culture, the country culture will take precedent.

As an example, **Appendix C** describes the former strong Newell culture and its cultural elements.

Ethics and Social Responsibility

We are all familiar with ethical issues associated with such companies as Enron, World Com, BP, Tyco, Arthur Andersen, and a variety of others. Serious ethical lapses and corrupt practices can destroy entire companies, placing entire work forces out on the street and devastating the financial base of communities. Today, we have new facts of business life. There will be more regulations like Sarbanes-Oxley. There will be more public and legal pressure on boards of directors and executives to behave in an ethical manner and placing the interest of shareholders first. And, environmental sustainability is clearly NOT a fad.

There is mounting evidence that companies who behave in a "green" manner are significantly outperforming their counterparts in terms of financial performance, public image, recruiting, and satisfaction and retention of employees. While there are a variety of definitions of being "green," I include three elements in my description of being a "green" company:

- Ethical
- Socially Responsible
- Environmentally Conscious

While it may seem controversial, my theorem of business social responsibility is:

"The number one social responsibility of business is to make a profit."

118

If a business is not profitable, it means loss of employment and job security, lack of opportunities for advancement, reduced or substandard compensation, elimination or reduction in health care and other benefits, reduced community tax revenues, declining community growth, loss of funding for education, limited economic growth, and no investment in the environment. On the other hand, if the company is profitable, it does have obligation to behave in a socially responsible manner and support these types of activities.

A thorny problem facing multinational companies is the prevalence of bribes and kickbacks common in many foreign environments. In Eastern Europe, for example, as much as 60% of all business transactions involve some form of bribery or kickback ranging from 2% to 8% of generated revenue. Many of the most common trading partners of U.S. companies have the highest incidence of global corruption, including Russia, Mexico, India, China, Mexico, and Brazil.   Companies who forbid payment of bribes face a formidable challenge in securing business where such payments are entrenched in local customs. Should we maintain a 'no bribery' stance, or should we follow local customs? What is in the best interest of shareholders? While many will disagree, my personal philosophy is shown in **Exhibit 13 – 4**. Please keep in mind that the Foreign Corrupt Practices ACT prohibits U.S. companies from paying bribes to **government officials and political candidates** in countries where they do business. It does not forbid such practices in non-governmental environments.

Exhibit 13 – 4   **Thomas Ethical Philosophy**
<ul><li>If illegal . . . Don't do it.</li><li>If unsure of legality . . . Don't do it.</li><li>If it damages employees, customers, the environment, etc. . . . Don't do it.</li><li>If it is immoral . . . Don't do it.</li><li>If it results in personal gain only . . . Don't do it.</li><li>If it is a gift . . . Accept only if it is locally customary AND the value is less than $50</li></ul> <div align="center">**Then ask . . .** **What are the common business practices?** **What is in the best interest of the stakeholders?**</div>

Does that mean the paying of bribes and kickbacks in cultures where it is standard business practice is permissible? The answer is a qualified 'yes' if it is the best interest of the stakeholders. The utilization of an outside middleman is preferred, where the third party is being paid a commission or finder's fee from which any bribes or kickbacks are paid. I would suggest that this philosophy can be best described as 'situational ethics."

I believe this is a typical philosophy among business leaders from the 'baby boomer' generation. There is increasing evidence that there are higher standards of ethical behavior in the future generation of leaders. It is also well-documented that female managers have higher ethical standards than males.

While we may disagree with ethical practices in foreign environments, we should not be too hasty in condemning these practices. For products sold in the United States, for example, it is unacceptable to market products from third world countries who are using child labor. In over one hundred countries, there are over 300,000 million children between the ages of five and fourteen who are working full time. In most cases, this is a necessity in order to assist in providing food and shelter for their families. How is this different from 100 years ago in the United States? As an example, my father, born in 1903, was the youngest of nine children and the only one to earn a high school diploma. Why? The children had to work on the farm in order for the family to survive. As countries become more and more integrated into international trade, labor, environmental, and safety standards evolve and the standard of living rises. Take, for instance, Taiwan. When I first traveled to Taiwan in the mid 1970's, I witnessed a great deal of child labor and deplorable working conditions. Today, Taiwan is one of the world's high tech centers, with a standard of living that is equivalent to Japan and educational attainment higher than that of the United States. Countries like China and Mexico are currently evolving in a similar fashion.

We face a variety of difficult ethical, social, and environmental decisions on a daily basis. Again, the evidence is quite clear that those companies with high levels of conduct codes who are ethical, socially responsible, and environmentally conscious will be the winners.

Chapter 14
Leadership . . . and the lessons from *'Good to Great'*

While some may contend that the subject of leadership is beyond the scope of this text, I believe superior leadership may be the most important characteristic in developing and implementing a successful business strategy. This contention is supported by the findings of the *'Good to Great'* study.

Jim Collins *'Good to Great'* was first published in 2001, and is the best-selling business-related book ever written. It was required reading for all my managers in a business setting, and was mandatory reading for students in all of my classes. Collins has subsequently published two follow-up books related to the findings of the *'Good to Great'* study. As an aside, I believe the second most important business applications book ever written was not really a business book at all . . . *'The Art of War'* written by Sun Tzu in the fourth century B.C.

Simply stated, the purpose of the study was to document why some companies were able to transition from 'good' performance to 'great' performance, while other companies, in the same industry with the same opportunities, did not. The questions Collins posed in developing the study were:

- Can a good company become great, and if so, how?
- What are the differences between companies that went from good to great versus those who did not?
- What characteristics did the good to great companies share?

Methodology

The *'Good to Great'* study was conducted by Collins over a five-year period while he was a professor at the University of Colorado – Boulder, using his MBA students as his research staff. It began with a six month financial analysis of over 1,400 companies to determine those companies who went from good to great results and sustained those results for at least a fifteen year period. The fifteen year criteria was established to eliminate any one hit wonders whose results were skewed due to explosive industry growth or technological breakthrough. Companies were chosen independent of industry, and were required to produce general stock market returns three times or greater than the market average. The initial 1,400 companies were then reduced to eleven companies who met these criteria. It is important to note the basis for study results was empirical evidence, NOT subjective conclusions or opinions as is the case for many authors.

Exhibit 14 - 1 lists the eleven good to great companies identified by Collins and his researchers and the eleven companies who operated in the same industry and had the same opportunities, but failed to produce outstanding results. In addition, he identified another eight companies (including Rubbermaid) who generated the required results, but could not sustain them for the fifteen year period. Please note that several companies, like Circuit City, subsequently failed. Collins addresses what happened to these companies, and others, in his follow-up publication *'How the Mighty Fall."*

Exhibit 14 -1
Good to Great Industries and Companies

Industry	Great Companies	Comparison Companies
• Medical Products	• Abbot	• Upjohn
• Appliances; Electronics	• Circuit City	• Silo
• Savings and Loans	• Fannie May	• Great Western
• Personal Care	• Gillette	• Warner – Lambert
• Paper Products	• Kimberly – Clark	• Scott Paper
• Retail Groceries	• Kroger	• A & P
• Steel	• Nucor	• Bethlehem Steel
• Tobacco; Consumables	• Philip Morris	• R.J. Reynolds
• Computers; Office Products	• Pitney Bowes	• Addressograph
• Drug Stores	• Walgreens	• Eckerd
• Regional Banks	• Wells Fargo	• Bank of America

There were a number of surprising results. First, the industries in which the great companies operated were not exciting, rapidly growing, or technology oriented. Second, it was expected the great companies would include names like IBM, WalMart, Coke, P&G, GE, Disney, etc. None of these companies met the study's criteria. In addition, there were a number of other surprises that were not included in the transition from good to great. There were no big name, celebrity leaders. There was no link to the level of executive compensation. There was an equal focus on what to do and what not to do. The companies were not technology driven. Mergers and acquisitions were not driving forces. The transition from good to great was a controlled process, rather than from a big event or 'magic moment."

#1 - Leadership

After detailed interviews with members of the eleven great companies and the 19 comparison and non-sustaining companies, the researchers submitted to Collins that the number one differentiating factor for the great companies was leadership. Collins essentially said "no" . . . he wanted to know the specific actions that drove the transition to great, not the people. So, the researchers were sent back to conduct more interviews and returned with same result . . . the quality of leadership was the most important variable to success.

Initial and subsequent interviews evidenced a clear difference between the leaders who drove their company from good to great and those who did not. **Exhibit 14 – 2** describes the common characteristics of the great leaders, whom Collins terms **Level 5 Leaders**. **Exhibit 14 – 3** outlines the common characteristics of the not-so-great leaders.

Exhibit 14 – 2 **Common Characteristics of the Great (Level 5) Leaders**
• Not highly egotistical. • Incredibly ambitious . . . for the company rather than themselves. • Company, not personal, success was first and foremost. • Intolerant of mediocrity . . . driven to produce outstanding results. • Organization members described the leader as "modest, humble, gracious, mild mannered, calm, fearless, and understated." • Frequently attributed success to "good luck." • Discussed success in terms of "we", rather than "I." • Low profile, limited publicity. • 10 of 11 came from within, versus outside, the company. • The window rather than the mirror. • Set up successors for success. • Not highly charismatic . . . inspiration came from the leader's overall vision and drive.

Exhibit 14 – 3 **Common Characteristics of the Comparison Leaders**
• Only two CEOs from the comparison and non-sustaining companies were internal. • More concerned with personal reputation and greatness than for company success. • Gargantuan personal egos. • Discussed success in terms of "I", rather than "we." • The 'Biggest Dog Syndrome' . . . set up successors for failure or chose weak successors. • Personal public relations . . . interviews, appearances, books. • Frequently attributed failure to "bad luck." • Were considered dictators. • The mirror rather than the window.

Several explanations are warranted. The concept of the 'window and the mirror' is particularly important. When performance was exceptional, the successful leader looked out the window and credited the success to other organization members. When things went poorly, this leader would look in the mirror and take personal responsibility for failures. Conversely, the failed leader looked in the mirror when things went well and credit himself for the success. When performance was poor, the CEO would look out the window and blame others in the organization, bad luck, industry softness, etc. for the failure.

The "biggest dog syndrome" refers to the leader who is willing to allow other dogs in the kennel, but had to be the biggest dog and make all important decisions, while not establishing a succession plan. A pre- Newell former CEO of Rubbermaid was described as "a genius with a 1,000 helpers". At the time of his departure, Rubbermaid was one of the most admired companies in the United States. When the CEO left the company, his hand-picked successor allowed company results to falter to the point of the Newell acquisition. At the time of the acquisition, the front cover of *Fortune* magazine described Rubbermaid as "from most admired to just acquired." After the Newell acquisition, the turnaround of Rubbermaid was slower than expected by the Board of Directors and a new, high-visibility CEO was appointed. He replaced most of the corporate and divisional management teams who had made the Newell organization successful, and brought his own "yes" executive team into the organization. The new CEO, who exhibited virtually all of the above traits of failed leadership, was able to drive company stock from a previous high of over $50 per share to under $10. A major business publication also extended him the dubious honor as one of the worst CEOs among the 500 largest U.S. public companies.

One of the surprises among these findings was the fact that ten of the eleven great leaders came from outside the organization, while 17 of 19 leaders from the comparison companies were external. This refutes the typical Board belief that they must hire larger-than-life personalities to transform companies. Some of these hires were larger-than-life failures that negatively correlated from going from good to great. In addition, there was also negative correlation between executive compensation and greatness. Yes, the great CEOs were well compensated and were paid based on performance, but not near the level of the big name hires. Nor were there high levels of guarantees or golden parachutes. Collins characterized the successful leaders as the type of people who would drive to excellence no matter how they were compensated.

Collins cites the career of Lee Iacocca as an example. Iacocca, following a 1980's bailout of Chrysler, did a fantastic job of turning around the company in the first half of his tenure. However, Chrysler stock trailed the market by over 30% in his second half. Why? He became more important than the company, appearing in over 80 commercials, having frequent appearances on the Today Show and Larry King Live, wrote a book that sold over seven million copies, married a new trophy wife, and entertained running for President. Rome was allowed to burn.

My favorite example is the former CEO of one of the comparison companies, who was successful in initially turning one of the comparison companies around until he left, and the house of cards collapsed. He then bankrupt a previously solid company in his next assignment. He named himself "Rambo in Pinstripes" and 'Chainsaw xxx." His publicity photographs were of him in a pinstripe suit, holding a chainsaw, and wearing a vest of bullets crisscrossing his chest. He then wrote a book and stated in the preface that he was to business what Michael Jordan was to basketball and Bruce Springsteen was to rock and roll. I witnessed his arrival at a major industry trade show, where he exited his limousine accompanied by two scantily clad young ladies who delivered him to his show booth. I (and Collins) contend this is not the type of leader who will motivate and rally the troops to achieve greatness.

Collins poses the questions "Can you become a great leader"? His answer is "Yes" with the following caveat:

> *"There is a category of people who never in a million years could bring themselves to subjugate their egoistic needs to building something larger and more lasting than themselves."*

#2 - First Who, Then What

While the number one finding deals with the quality of people in leadership roles, number two also deals with the human element of the people within the organization. The straightforward elements of the 'First Who, Then What' concept is:

- **Get the right people on the bus**
- **Get the wrong people off the bus**
- **Get the right people in the right seats**
- **Then figure out where to drive the bus**

The translation from a strategic standpoint is, therefore, once you have the right people in the right seats, only then can you develop and implement a winning strategy.

Letting the wrong people staff the organization is unfair to the right people and it is ultimately unfair to the wrong people, who will not be satisfied with their jobs and careers. You need to get the wrong people off the bus NOW. Be rigorous, but don't be ruthless. If you fail to act on the underperformers, you will lose the respect and confidence of your superiors, peers, and subordinates and your career advancement will be compromised. Having the right people in the organization will result in vigorous debate and create healthy conflict in search of the best answers and courses of action. An organization void of conflict is destined to apathy and mediocrity. The right people has more to do with personal traits than with specific knowledge, background and skills. The right people first and foremost must have intelligence and drive . . . they can learn the business quickly.

There is another important lesson from *Good to Great* that I did not learn during my career . . . "Put the best people on the biggest opportunities, NOT the biggest problems." When WalMart or Home Depot had significant issues, I elected to throw the entire organization around solving the issue. As a result, I am confident that a number of revenue and profit opportunities in other areas were missed. By way of example, at one time, Philip Morris domestic sales represented 99% of revenue, while non-North American business represented only 1%. The head of their domestic tobacco business was offered the opportunity to move to lead the international business only . . . on the surface a career demotion. The executive accepted the assignment and, in a handful of years, made Marlboro the number one worldwide brand of cigarettes.

Other Findings

- **Confront the Brutal Facts (and never lose faith)**

    You cannot change the course of a business without facing reality. A climate of trust and truth must prevail in order to attack the realities head-on. Embrace and encourage the messengers . . . don't shoot them. Consider the steps in developing the strategy. Three-fourths of the time is spent understanding and analyzing the business in order to develop a successful strategy and action plans. And, once you have the brutal facts, the strategy is often self-evident.

- **Simplicity Within the Three Circles**

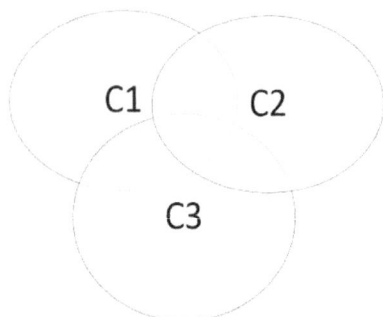

Consider the three circles above where:

> C1 = What can you be best in the world at?
> > If you can't be the best, you can't be great.
> > It's equally important to understand what you can't be best at.
> > May mean departing core or long-term businesses.
>
> C2 = What drives your economic engine?
>
> C3 = What are you deeply passionate about?

The intersection of these three circles in the one big thing that the company does best and they must stick to it! Tom Peters termed it "stick to your knitting" in *In Search of Excellence.* Should WalMart enter the hospital management market or the production of defense aircraft? I think not! Do not be lured by once in a lifetime opportunities that takes your human and financial resources off the one big thing, like Circuit City did with the acquisition of Car Max.

- **A Culture of Discipline**

    Formal and bureaucratic cultures attempt to compensate for having the wrong people on the bus and a lack of discipline in staying within the intersection of the three circles. If you have the right people in the right seats, you do not need an excessive hierarchy and rules. Discipline also means the 'stop doing list' is just as important as the 'to do' list.

- **Building Momentum**

    The good to great companies moved slowly forward at first, then built momentum over time. The transformation was a cumulative process, with no single defining event or action, grand program, miracle moment or killer breakthrough. From outside the company, the transformation appeared revolutionary. But, from inside the company, it appeared to be a natural evolutionary process. Acquisitions did not drive the transformation and were undertaken only after momentum was being built. None of the good to great companies were technology creators or used technology to transform the company. Technology was only used selectively to assist or accelerate the transition.

    In contrast, the comparison companies ended up in what Collins termed the "doom loop," where management would attempt to go directly in a new direction without any build of momentum. New leadership takes over and immediately attempts to go in a new direction with radical change, a major acquisition, the embracing of fads, lots of hoopla, etc. The result was no accumulation of momentum and disappointing results, which leads to a new management team being brought in and the whole "doom loop" process starts over.

    The lessons of *Good to Great*, particularly in terms of leadership and human resources, is certainly enlightening and does not take a team of Harvard MBAs to implement. The bottom line is simply good common sense management . . . common business sense and behavior that certainly does not prevail in many organizations. However, if you investigate some of the most dynamic and well-run companies in today's business environment, you will surely find the lessons from *Good to Great* are present.

    Next, is a brief review of Collins' two subsequent publications, both of which support that, if the lessons of *Good to Great* are followed, the likelihood of success will be significantly enhanced.

How the Mighty Fall

    In 2009, Collins published *How the Mighty Fall*, a study of how one time great companies decline and, in many cases, disappear, including the previously heralded Circuit City. As shown in **Exhibit 14 - 4**, there are five identified stages of decline, which can happen quickly or transpire over a period of decades. The decline of Rubbermaid occurred in less than five years prior to Newell's acquisition. The demise of

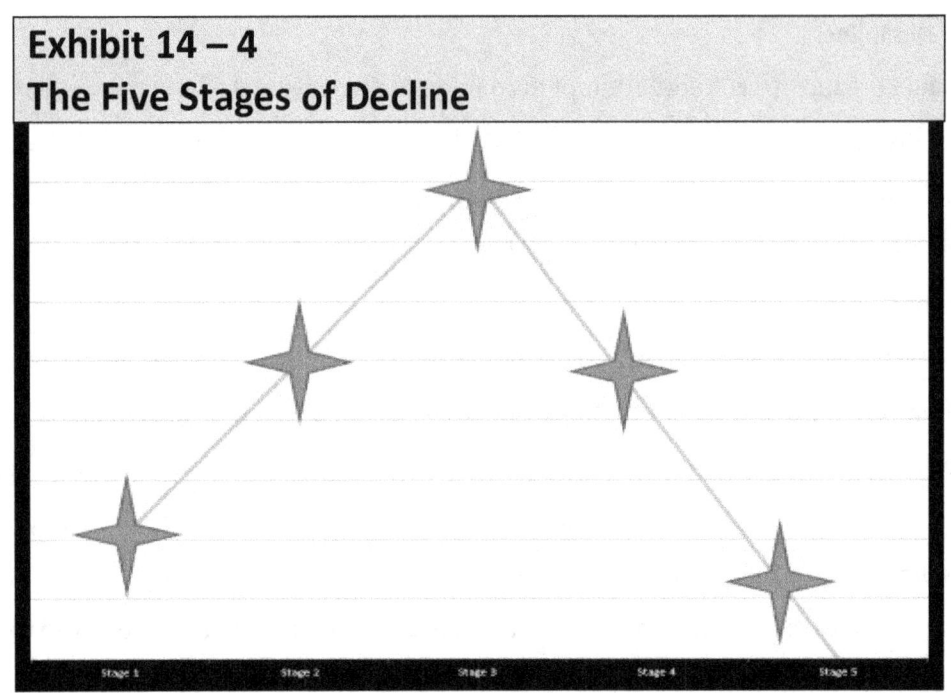

Exhibit 14 – 4
The Five Stages of Decline

Stage 1   Stage 2   Stage 3   Stage 4   Stage 5

A&P grocery stores and Zenith home electronics, the once largest firms in their respective industries, occurred over a period of several decades. These stages are:

Stage 1: Arrogance and Invulnerability
Usually breed by previous success; failure to respond to changes in the market, demand, and/or competition.

Stage 2: Undisciplined Pursuit of More
Confusing big with great; growth for the sake of growth; expanding outside current competencies; bold acquisitions; only one of the studied firms was complacent in growing their business.

Stage 3: Denial of Risk and Peril
Failure to confront the brutal facts; the data must be wrong; gross margins eroding, excess inventory; management simply not paying attention.

Stage 4: Grasping for Salvation
Searching for the silver bullet to turn the arrow; obsessive reorganization, frequent strategy changes; significant financial deterioration.

Stage 5: Irrelevance or Death
Lack of cash; the only remaining question is whether to continue to fight or capitulate.

The real question comes is stage four . . . can companies grasping for salvation turn the arrow and become a great company? The answer is "Yes" . . . Apple from the mid 1990's versus today is the most dramatic example. Others include IBM, Disney, Texas Instruments, and Boeing. How have they done it? In virtually all instances, it was implementing the lessons learned in *Good to Great* . . . Level 5 leadership, getting the right people on the bus, confronting the brutal facts, developing a culture of discipline, and consistent building of momentum.

Great by Choice

As a consequence of the 2008-2009 recession and turmoil, Collins undertook a historical study to learn how companies produce spectacular results in turbulent and chaotic environments. For example, Southwest Airlines has continue to grow and generate strong profitability, while many of their competitors have been in and out of Chapter 11 or now reside in the airline graveyard. Since 1972, Southwest faced an oil crisis and embargo, hyperinflation, deregulation, controller strikes, and 9/11. During the 2008-2009 recession, they were the only U.S. airline to generate profits. Between 1980 and 2002, Apple trailed the stock market by 80%. We are all aware of Apple's progress since that time . . . one of the greatest turnarounds in U.S. business history. Collins described these firms as the 10x companies, those that beat their industry index by at least ten times. How did these companies, and a number of others, operate successfully during these periods of turmoil?

1. **Leadership**

   It should come as no surprise that the leaders exhibited the same characteristics as those found in the *Good to Great* study. Enough said.

2. **Consistent Performance**

   The 10x companies set a minimum level of acceptable performance AND a self-imposed upper limit that they would not exceed. This relates to a culture of discipline and a conservative build of momentum, also a finding of *Good to Great*.

3. **Disciplined Innovation and Empirical Creativity**

   Collins uses the analogy of firing bullets not cannonballs. Rather than using all your ammunition to fire one big cannonball, which results in failure if you miss, fire bullets to first ensure you have your target in range. Then use the remaining ammunition to fire the cannonball. It is also pointed out that copying is not a sin. Apple's success is not necessarily associated with revolutionary innovation, in many cases it was taking existing technology and making spectacular adaptations and improvements.

4. **Live Above the Death Line**

   "The only mistakes you learn from are the ones you survive." Prepare for unexpected "Black Swan" events, build cash reserves and financial buffers, and embark on cautious risk-taking. In Collins study, he found only 22% of the major decisions made in the 10x companies were described as high risk. Among comparison companies in the same industries who were unsuccessful during turbulent times, 43% of decisions were categorized as high risk.

5. **SMaC**

Company strategies and decisions were SMaC . . . specific, methodical, and consistent. Over time, the 10x companies changed only an average of 15% of their strategic objectives, compared to 60% of their unsuccessful peers. As an example, Southwest Airlines included the following elements in their initial strategy, only one of which (Texas priority) is not a current strategic element.

- Short hauls, point-to-point, and under two hour routes
- 737 aircraft only (common parts and service requirements)
- Rapid turnarounds
- Passenger vs. air freight focus
- No food service
- No interlining (no baggage transfer to other airlines)
- Employees are family
- Texas #1 priority

Another interesting example of SMaC is the U.S. Constitution . . . since 1791, there have been only 17 new amendments to our Constitution.

In closing, a couple of quotes from Collins are worth citing:

"The root cause of how one becomes great and the other does not cannot be circumstance or luck. The factors that determine whether or not a company becomes great, even in a chaotic and uncertain world, lie largely within the hands of its people."

"It's what you do before the storm comes that most determines how well you'll do when the storm does come."

Appendix A
Strategic Plan Format

Company:

Date:

1. BUSINESS OVERVIEW

Aggregate Market:

Participating Market:

Business Definition:

Macro Business Environment:
       Economic:
       Demographic:
       Socio-Culture:
       Political and Legal:
       Technological:
       Global:

2. MARKET ENVIRONMENT

Industry Environment:

Competitive Environment:

Five Forces Model:
       Intensity of Rivalry:
       Threat of New Entrants:
       Bargaining Power of Buyers/End Users:
       Bargaining Power of Suppliers:
       Threat of Substitutes:
       Impact of Compliments:

Industry Key Success Factors:

Industry Attractiveness:

3. COMPANY INTERNAL ENVIRONMENT

Internal Financial Analysis:
       Financials Over Time:
       Trends and Comments:

External Financial Analysis:
        Competitive Financial Comparisons:
        Comments:

Sales and Product Analysis:

Value Chain Benchmarking/Best Practices:

4. SWOT ANALYSIS

Competitive Matrix:

Strengths:

Weaknesses:

Opportunities:

Threats:

Immediate Action Requirements:

5. STRATEGIC OVERVIEW

Strategic Positioning (Low Cost, Differentiation, or Best Value):

Broad or Focused Market:

Company Vision Statement:

Company Mission Statement:

New Business Definition (if appropriate):

6. STRATEGIC OBJECTIVES

OBJECTIVE 1 (Revenue):
        Action Plan:
        Timetable:

OBJECTIVE 2 (Profitability)
        Action Plan:
        Timetable:

OBJECTIVE 3 (Financial or Market-Driven):
        Action Plan:
        Timetable:

OBJECTIVE 4 (Financial or Market-Driven):
        Action Plan:
        Timetable:

ETC.:

Appendix B
Anatomy of a Successful Acquisition

As previously presented, Newell's primary growth vehicle was the acquisition of underperforming companies who had a strong market share position, and turning them into successful ventures. One such example was the acquisition of the Kirsch Company from Cooper Industries. Kirsch and Newell Window Furnishings, at the time, were the number one and two leaders in the North American stock non-textile window treatment industry. Both companies were approximately $150 million in annual revenue. In addition, Kirsch also generated $60+ million from their European window treatment business unit, as well as having several struggling non-related business which were jettisoned. While the European business unit was fairly profitable, the domestic business was generating a 5% operating loss. Conversely, Newell Window Furnishings was generating an operating profit in excess of 15%. Accordingly, if the businesses were just combined with no consolidation efforts, operating profit would have been in the 4% range. My challenge was, therefore, to turn around Kirsch performance and consolidate the two North American businesses to make **1 + 1 = 3.**

Pre – Acquisition Planning

While we were confident the acquisition would be approved, intervention from the Department of Justice regarding potential monopoly creation claims of a competitor slowed the finalization of the acquisition by about 90 days. Since I was involved in the due diligence process, I had a great deal of knowledge of financial, market, and organization details of the company. However, until the acquisition was approved by the DOJ and consummated between Newell and Cooper Industries, a gag order did not allow me to share the information and knowledge I had attained.

Job number one, therefore, was to assemble a management team capable of consolidating the acquisition, while ensuring no performance erosion at Newell Window Furnishings. This included four Vice Presidents from the existing business, one from another Newell Company, and one from outside the organization with whom I had previous experience. As will be discussed later, the primary reason the acquisition and subsequent consolidation was so successful was the world class team that was assembled. It should be noted that within 24 months following the acquisition, all members of the team, including myself, were promoted to other Newell operating divisions or corporate assignments.

The second priority was, with the information obtained in the due diligence process, to develop a preliminary mission statement and business strategy, which could not be shared with the new management team due to the imposed gag order. One week before securing the keys to the new company, we were finally able to review the materials that I had assembled and begin the process of outlining formal strategic objectives and action plans. At the outset, our mission statement was:

Consolidate Kirsch North American operations earning minus 5% operating

income with Newell Window Furnishings with 15% operating income

into a single entity earning 10% (15%) or greater with 24 months,

with no major loss of business.

We, as a team, established the goal of achieving 15% within 18 months. Our commitment to corporate headquarters, however, was generate 10% within 24 months. Why the difference? My rule of budgeting and commitment is to "under promise and over deliver." Had we committed to 15% and achieved only 12%, we failed. However, if we committed to 10% and achieved 12%, we would be regarded as winners. In actuality, we did achieve 15.4% in the first full year following the acquisition and consolidation.

For six months following the acquisition, our team essentially lived in the Kirsch "guest house" in southern Michigan, traveling back to Illinois most weekends. Our daily schedule was typically in the headquarters office or main factory from 7:00 a.m. to 7:00 p.m. followed by dinner and discussing until late in the evening our daily findings and observations. Essentially, we updated and changed the originally developed strategy on a daily basis. Day to day activities and decisions at Newell Window Furnishings operations in Illinois were handled predominately by the functional area managers (and they did a terrific job . . . performance actually improved without us!). There was very little overlap of business as Newell's key customers were WalMart and Home Depot, while Kirsch's key customers were upscale department stores, decorating centers, and J.C. Penney (their #1 customer).

Strategic Objectives and Action Plans

In order to turn around and consolidate the businesses, the objectives and action requirements were numerous as outlined on the next few pages.

Objective: Restate financials to Newell accounting standards; rebudget balance of year forecast; install Newell systems and controls.
> **Timeline:** NOW!
> **Results/Comments:** Completed in 30 days.

Objective: Replace Kirsch executive management; assess others to determine future organization.
> **Timeline:** Executive management terminated day #1; three months assessment of others.
> **Results/Comments:** While removal of Kirsch's executive team may sound harsh, our belief was that the same team who drove the company to unprofitable results and erosion of market share is NOT the team that will turn the company around. One key executive was left in place, and that proved to be a mistake.

Objective: No major customer losses.

    Timeline: Ongoing

    Results/Comments: One major Kirsch customer lost (our decision); $3 million erosion in unprofitable small account direct sale business; President and VP Sales met with top 10 customers within first 30 days to assure they understood the improvements that were forthcoming.

Objective: Renew emphasis on new products.

    Timeline: Immediate

    Results/Comments: Since the company had been for sale for 18 months, no new product development was undertaken, which was the historic cornerstone of company success; over 50 new products were introduced within the first year following the acquisition.

Objective: Leverage and consolidate suppliers.

    Timeline: 120 days

    Results/Comments: Through the power of the consolidated companies, suppliers of common materials and services were leveraged for lower prices and better terms. Vendor consolidation resulted in a 5% savings on common inputs.

Objective: Increase Kirsch outsourcing versus vertical integration.

    Timeline: 180 days

    Results/Comments: Kirsch overly vertically integration; outsourcing of several activities resulted in significant cost savings.

Objective: Asset control . . . increase inventory turns to 4.0 (vs. 2.5); dispose of excess and obsolete; attack DSO and DPO; eliminate slow moving SKUs.

    Timeline: 180 days

    Results/Comments: Accomplished; poor asset management is a typical issue with underperforming companies.

Objective: Discontinue direct sales to small decorator accounts with under $2,500 in annual purchases; replace with regional distributors.

    Timeline: 180 days

    Results/Comments: Company losing approximately 15% on small customers; loss of approximately $3 million in sales, with remaining $7 million profitable.

Objective: Consolidate/close underutilized manufacturing and/or distribution facilities.

    Timeline: One year

    Results/Comments: Six U.S. and two Canadian facilities closed within eight months with no lawsuits or work stoppages; production and distribution moved to main Illinois and Michigan facilities.

Objective: Consolidate headquarters

    Timeline: One year

    Results/Comments: Headquarters moved to Illinois nine months after acquisition; handful of former Kirsch middle managers relocated.

Objective: Consolidate manufacturing and primary distribution to Illinois, Michigan, or offshore.

    Timeline: Two years

    Results/Comments: Michigan UAW facilities closed at 18 months; high automation manufacturing to Illinois; new Illinois leased distribution facility constructed; high labor content manufacturing to newly established Mexico facility or China suppliers; 500+ workers displaced.

Objective: Displaced employee support.

Timeline: Ongoing

Results/Comments: The most disturbing part of the acquisition and subsequent actions was the displacement of 700-800 former Kirsch employees, many of whom had been with the company for many years. We provided reasonable severance packages, stay bonuses where applicable, extended benefits, on-site placement assistance, psychological support where necessary, and local networking. While displaced employees were angry over job loss, we were at least credited with treating these employees with dignity and compassion, which resulted in no legal actions and associated expenses.

Obviously this was an extremely successful acquisition and turnaround. I believe this can be attributed to two primary variables:

1. **The Strategy**

   We developed a clear, participative and dynamic strategy, which was modified on a virtual daily basis as our management team became involved and knowledgeable about the organization, markets and customers, issues, etc.

2. **The People**

   The single most significant factor that drove the success of this venture was the world class team assembled to lead the turn around and consolidation. We had . . .

   - The right people on the bus
   - The right people in the right seats
   - The wrong people removed from the bus
   - The right people given the ball to run with

In actuality, I had the easiest job of all. I simply was the traffic director . . . ensuring that we were all shooting at the same targets, encouraging rigorous debate and disagreement (which often got quite heated), and keeping the corporate office appraised of our activities. Thanks to Rich, Joe, Mari Lyn, Greg ('Eddie Munster'), Mike, Jeff ('Boog'), and Billy for not allowing me to screw it up. It should be noted that all of these leaders were promoted to new positions in Newell within 18 months of the acquisition.

Appendix C
A Strong Culture Example . . . Newell

For many years, Newell conducted 'Newell University' once or twice per year for two days in a centralized location. All new managers and professionals, both from existing business and new acquisitions, were required to participate. The purpose of these sessions was to educate newcomers regarding the operating and managerial philosophies of corporation. Included in the agenda was a presentation of Newell's "15 Commandments," which communicated the organization's culture and how each of its varied free-standing business units should be managed. Following is an abbreviated overview of those commandments.

Commandment #1: Create a sense of urgency climate.

Complacent businesses without a sense of urgency fail. Do it now, not when we get around to doing it. Speed is life!

Commandment #2: Create a profit intensive posture.

We are in business to make money. The creation of careers, the presence of jobs, fulfillment of social responsibilities, and health and other benefits would be nonexistent with profitability (as I presented earlier in Chapter 13).

Commandment #3: Hands-on divisional leadership.

Managers must be 100% committed to and take ownership in the business. Companies with many layers of management and rigid organizational boundaries are businesses that wander and fail.

Commandment #4: Exceptional people . . . develop and delegate.

Recruit and hire only the best! We want only the smartest, the brightest, the quickest, and most dedicated to fill our organization. Then we must delegate to these qualified people and hold them accountable. If we wish to continue to be successful, we need to develop most of our future leaders internally . . . people who have proven they can make it in the Newell environment.

Commandment #5: Strong distaste for mediocrity.

Average is not good enough, we have to be the best. If we begin to rest and allow average to be good enough, when we meet our competition they will win.

Commandment #6: Strong dislike for competitors.

"Dislike" may be too gentle a term. "Hate" and "Despise" may be more appropriate. Competitors only take away from you the food from your table, the car from your garage, your bonus, and ultimately your career opportunities.

Commandment #7: Merchandise the difference.

It's the difference that sells. Not to differentiate is to give in to becoming a commodity, to being a follower, and an also-ran. Keep looking for new differences that set you apart from your competition.

Commandment #8: Consistent market share growth.

If you're not growing, you are dying! Being number one in a market isn't good enough, we need to find new and innovative ways to both grow the market and secure business from our competitors.

Commandment #9: Top management must be highly visible in the market.

In all managerial positions, we must be visible in the marketplace and with our customers. This is especially true for division Presidents, who are each company's chief marketing officer.

Commandment #10: If it is a good idea, do it now.

Don't get caught by the paralysis by analysis syndrome. A good idea may only be good today. Take a chance, take a risk, and do it today before your competition does.

Commandment #11: Be the low cost global provider.

Whether we manufacture product or source it, we must be the low cost producer, marketer, seller, distributor, bill collector, financier, and information provider.

Commandment #12: When business is soft, do something about it, even if it may not work.

Albert Einstein was credited with saying "True insanity is doing the same thing over and over and over again while expecting different results." Doing something about a soft business is a must, even if it does not work. Complacency leads to failure.

Commandment #13: No surprise mandate.

If something negative is developing, get it out in the open and get people involved. Only then can the problem be solved. Attack the problem before it becomes a surprise and don't shoot the messenger.

Commandment #14: Budget discipline.

Your budget is your contract and the blueprint for managing your business. If you are not on budget in terms of sales, costs, or expenses, do whatever it takes to get back on your budget and make the numbers.

Commandment #15: The divisional President sets the pace.

If your President goes left, the company goes left. If the President slows down or speeds up, so does the company. If the President bitches or makes excuses, so will others in the company. Trees die from the top!

Please note, Commandment #5 suggests Newell business units strive to have a **Differentiation Strategy,** while Commandment #11 relates to a **Low Cost Strategy**. Accordingly, the actual generic strategy across all business units is a **Best Value Strategy** . . . a combination of low costs (not necessarily low prices) and product and marketing differentiation.

These commandments define the former culture of Newell and drove its success in the marketplace and with investors. It should be recognized that not all employees or prospective employees can thrive in this type of culture, which defines why the company administered intelligence and personality tests, followed by in-depth interviews with an industrial psychologist. It helped ensure that the company culture and the person's individual culture were compatible.

Bibliography

Jim Collins, *Good to Great: How Some Companies Make the Leap . . . and Others Don't* (New York: HarperCollins Publishers, Inc., 2001).

Jim Collins, *How the Mighty Fall: And Why Some Companies Never Give In* (New York: HarperCollins Publishers, Inc., 2009).

Jim Collins and Morten T. Hansen, *Great by Choice* (New York: HarperCollins Publishers, Inc., 2011).

Dr. Robert Katz, Newell Board of Directors, *Newell Divisional Strategy Content.*

Thomas J. Peters and Robert H. Waterman, Jr., *In Search of Excellence: Lessons from America's Best-Run Companies* (New York: Harper and Row Publishers, Inc., 1982).

General Colin Powell, Chairman (Ret.) Joint Chief of Staff. Secretary of State (Ret.), *A Leadership Primer* (AHMA Presentation, Chicago, 1997).

Stephen P. Robbins and Timothy A. Judge, *Organizational Behavior*, 14th Edition (New Jersey: Pearson Education, Inc., 2011).

Sun Tzu (Edited and Foreword by James Clavell), *The Art of War* (New York: Bantam Doubleday Dell Publishing Group, Inc., 1983).

Arthur A. Thompson, Margaret A, Peteraf, John E. Gamble, and A.J. Strickland III, *Crafting and Executing Strategy: The Quest for Competitive Advantage*, 18th Edition (New York: McGraw/Hill Irwin, 2012).

John J. Wild and Kenneth L Wild, *International Business: The Challenges of Globalization*, 6th Edition (New Jersey: Pearson Education, Inc., 2012).